Soups

A Pyramid Cookery Paperback

Soups

hamlyn

An Hachette Livre UK Company
www.hachettelivre.co.uk

A Pyramid Paperback

First published in Great Britain in 2004 by
Hamlyn, a division of Octopus Publishing
Group Ltd,
2–4 Heron Quays, London E14 4JP
www.octopusbooks.co.uk

This edition published 2008

Copyright © Octopus Publishing Group Ltd
2004, 2008

ISBN 978-0-600-61764-8

A CIP catalogue record for this book is available
from the British Library

Printed and bound in China

10 9 8 7 6 5 4 3 2 1

Notes

Both metric and imperial measurements
are given for the recipes. Use one set of
measures only, not a mixture of both.

Ovens should be preheated to the
specified temperature. If using a fan-
assisted oven, follow the manufacturer's
instructions for adjusting the time and
temperature. Grills should also be preheated.

This book includes dishes made with nuts
and nut derivatives. It is advisable for those
with known allergic reactions to nuts and
nut derivatives and those who may be
potentially vulnerable to these allergies,
such as pregnant and nursing mothers,
invalids, the elderly, babies and children, to
avoid dishes made with nuts and nut oils. It
is also prudent to check the labels of
preprepared ingredients for the possible
inclusion of nut derivatives.

Fresh herbs should be used unless
otherwise stated. If unavailable use dried
herbs as an alternative but halve the
quantities stated.

Contents

Introduction

Piping hot, cool and chilled, light and healthy, hearty and nutritious, rich and creamy or sumptuous and sophisticated — soup comes in a thousand different forms. But there's one thing that every bowl of soup has in common — it's always a treat. Whether you're looking for the perfect comfort food or the ultimate health-kick, you will always find it in a bowl of soup.

A quick history

Soup has been eaten for millennia, ever since early man first discovered how to make vessels in which to boil food. The earliest soups were probably a by-product of cooking other foods in liquid — but since nothing was wasted in those times, the cooking broth was eaten too.

Today, every nation has their own soups — sup, zuppe, shorba, sopa, pho to name but a few. In Greece they eat egg and lemon Avgolemono; in Southeast Asia they enjoy fiery, fragrant broths, and creamy concoctions made with coconut milk. In Morocco the national soup is Harira, made of beans and lentils, which is favoured during the month-long fast of Ramadan. In Russia it is Borscht — served chunky or smooth, hot or cold, but always a vibrant purplish-red.

Classic soups are constantly evolving, being re-invented each time different cultures and cuisines collide. Mulligatawny was adopted and adapted by the British stationed in India during colonial times, while many Vietnamese soups show a distinct French influence. Modern chefs love to take old recipes such as Venetian Risi e Bisi and Hungarian Goulash and transform them into new and utterly delicious soups.

Getting started

Soups are one of the easiest dishes to make and all the recipes in this book are simple to prepare and cook. All you need is a chopping board and knife, a large saucepan for cooking and a wooden spoon for stirring. If the soup needs to be blended, a blender or food processor is invaluable. However, many soups can be puréed using a mouli or food mill, and coarse-textured vegetable soups can often be achieved simply by using a potato masher.

Perfect results

The key to a good soup is using good-quality ingredients, and the most important ingredient of all is stock. Stock forms the base of almost every soup, and it is upon this that all the other flavours build. A poor-quality stock can spoil a soup, no matter how delicious the other ingredients are. It is best to use fresh, homemade stock (see recipes on pages 8–11). However, you can also buy excellent fresh stocks in supermarkets. Stock cubes and stock powders make a good storecupboard standby, but buy a good-quality brand as the flavour can vary enormously.

Time-savers

• Fresh stock can be stored in the freezer, so it's well worth keeping a batch at the ready. Make a large amount and freeze in several smaller containers so that you can defrost one quantity at a time.

- Another great time-saver is using canned pulses instead of dried. If using pulses in brine, rinse well and taste the soup before adding extra salt.
- When buying meat, fish or shellfish, ask for it to be prepared for you ready for cooking, where possible.

Freezing soups

It can be useful to make a double batch of soup and freeze half for another day. As a general rule, smooth and chunky vegetable soups freeze well. Delicate broths containing tofu and noodles, and soups containing shellfish and eggs, will not freeze successfully. To freeze soups containing cream and cheese, it is best to freeze the soup before these ingredients are added; stir them into the soup once it has been defrosted and reheated. Fresh herbs and garnishes should always be added at the last minute, never frozen in the soup.

The finishing touch

When it comes to serving soup, presentation is everything. The same bowl of tomato soup can make a comforting meal when you're ill, a hearty and nutritious supper on a cold winter evening or a stunning dish for entertaining, depending on how you present it. For convalescence, serve it plain and piping hot; for sustenance, scatter over strips of frazzled bacon and grated cheese and serve with chunks of crusty bread; and for sophistication, ladle the soup into elegant soup plates, add a swirl of cream and scatter over fresh basil leaves.

Soups can be garnished in a hundred different ways. Simplest of all are fresh herbs; go for classic flavour combinations such as carrot and coriander, or spinach and dill. Spices such as paprika can make a good garnish too. Dress up Asian-style soups with shreds of spring onion and fiery chilli, or top Mediterranean-style soups with shavings of Parmesan cheese. Crunchy fried shallots, colourful vegetable crisps or tortilla chips make a great alternative to the classic croûton, and a spoonful of tangy salsa or fragrant pesto can make a sensational change to the traditional dollop of cream. When you're choosing a garnish, the golden rule is be creative and, above all, have fun!

Vegetable stock

makes **about 1.8 litres (3 pints)**
preparation time **15 minutes**
cooking time **2½–3 hours**

1.8 litres (3 pints) water
1 onion, unpeeled and halved
1 garlic clove, unpeeled and halved
1 carrot, roughly chopped
1 celery stick with leaves, roughly
    chopped
¼ small swede, unpeeled and
    roughly chopped
1 leek, white and green parts,
    roughly chopped
1 parsley sprig
6 black peppercorns
1 bay leaf
1 bouquet garni
peelings of 1–2 scrubbed potatoes
outer leaves of cauliflower,
    cabbage, Brussels sprouts
    (optional)
salt

1 Combine the measured water with all the remaining ingredients in a deep saucepan. Bring to the boil, then lower the heat and simmer, covered, for 2½–3 hours. Skim off the scum with a slotted spoon from time to time.

2 Cool, then strain through a sieve, discarding all the vegetables and herbs in the sieve. Cover the stock closely and store in the refrigerator. Use within 3–4 days. This stock is suitable for freezing; if frozen, use within 4 months.

Chicken stock

makes **3.6 litres (6 pints)**
preparation time **5–8 minutes**
cooking time **2½–3 hours**

1 whole chicken carcass
3.6 litres (6 pints) water
1 teaspoon salt
1 Spanish onion, peeled and stuck
   with 4 cloves
2 celery sticks, chopped
2 carrots, roughly chopped
2 parsley sprigs
1 bouquet garni
1 bay leaf
8 black peppercorns

1 Put the carcass into a deep saucepan, cover with the measured water and add the salt. Bring to the boil, skimming off the scum with a slotted spoon. Lower the heat, partially cover the pan and simmer for 1 hour.

2 Add the onion, celery, carrots, parsley, bouquet garni, bay leaf and peppercorns. Stir and continue simmering, partially covered, for a further $1\frac{1}{2}$–2 hours. Add more water if the level drops below the bones.

3 Cool slightly. Remove the carcass, then strain the stock through a fine sieve into a bowl, discarding all the vegetables and herbs. After straining the stock, pick over the carcass, remove any meat still on the bones and add it to the stock.

4 Leave to cool, then skim off the fat with a spoon or blot with kitchen paper. Cover the stock closely and store in the refrigerator. Use within 3 days. This stock is suitable for freezing; if frozen, use within 3 months.

Fish stock

makes **1 litre (1¾ pints)**
preparation time **5–8 minutes**
cooking time **30–40 minutes**

500 g (1 lb) fish trimmings (bones, heads, tails, skins)
900 ml (1½ pints) water
1 onion, quartered
2 celery sticks with leaves, roughly chopped
1 bay leaf
1 parsley sprig
¼ teaspoon salt
6 black peppercorns
150 ml (¼ pint) dry white wine or cider

1 Put the fish trimmings into a large saucepan and cover with the measured water. Add all the remaining ingredients, stir well and bring to the boil, skimming off the scum as it rises to the surface with a slotted spoon. Lower the heat and simmer, partially covered, for 30–40 minutes.

2 Remove the saucepan from the heat and strain the mixture through a sieve, discarding the fish trimmings and other ingredients. Cool, then cover closely and store in the refrigerator. Use within 2 days. This stock is suitable for freezing; if frozen, use within 2 months.

tip The heads, tails and bones of white fish, such as cod, haddock, plaice, hake or whiting, make a good stock, but oily fish like mackerel and herring are not suitable.

Beef stock

makes **3.6 litres (6 pints)**
preparation time **15 minutes**
cooking time **about 4 hours**

about 1 kg (2 lb) marrow and
   skin bones
3.6 litres (6 pints) water
1 teaspoon salt
1 onion, quartered
2 celery sticks with leaves,
   roughly chopped
2 carrots, roughly chopped
4 parsley sprigs
1 bouquet garni
8 black peppercorns

1 Put the bones into a large saucepan. Cover them with the measured water and add the salt. Bring the liquid to the boil, skimming off any scum that rises to the surface with a slotted spoon. Lower the heat, partially cover the pan and simmer over a low heat for 2 hours. Skim from time to time.

2 Add the remaining ingredients and continue to simmer for a further 2 hours. Add more water if the level drops below the bones.

3 Cool slightly, then strain the stock through a fine sieve into a bowl, discarding the bones, vegetables, herbs and spices. Leave the stock to cool, then skim off the fat with a spoon or blot with kitchen paper. Cover the stock closely and store in the refrigerator. Use within 3 days. This stock is suitable for freezing; if frozen, use within 3 months.

Quick and Easy Soups

Simple, healthy and requiring minimal time in the kitchen, these soups are the ultimate convenience food. The recipes in this chapter are ideal for light lunches, afterwork snacks or impromptu meals for unexpected visitors.

Broccoli and cheese soup

serves **6**
preparation time **20 minutes**
cooking time **35–40 minutes**

1 kg (2 lb) broccoli
50 g (2 oz) butter
1 onion, chopped
1 large potato, peeled and
   quartered
1.5 litres (2½ pints) Vegetable
   Stock (see page 8)
125 ml (4 fl oz) single cream
1 tablespoon lemon juice
1 teaspoon Worcestershire sauce
a few drops of Tabasco sauce,
   or to taste
125 g (4 oz) mature Cheddar,
   grated
salt and pepper
watercress sprigs, to garnish

1 Remove all the tough stems and leaves from the broccoli. Cut off the stalks, peel them and cut them into 2.5 cm (1 inch) pieces. Break the florets into very small pieces and set them aside.

2 Melt the butter in a large saucepan. Add the onion and broccoli stalks and cook, covered, for 5 minutes over a moderate heat, stirring frequently.

3 Add the reserved broccoli florets, potato and stock to the pan. Bring the mixture to the boil. Cook, partially covered, for 5 minutes. Season the mixture to taste with salt and pepper and continue to cook over a moderate heat for 20 minutes, or until all the vegetables are soft.

4 Using a blender or food processor, purée the mixture until smooth, then transfer to a clean saucepan. Add the cream, lemon juice, Worcestershire sauce and Tabasco to the pan. Simmer for 3–5 minutes. Do not allow to boil or the soup will curdle. Just before serving, stir in the grated cheese and garnish each portion with watercress sprigs.

Parsnip and fennel soup

serves **4–6**
preparation time **10–15 minutes**
cooking time **35–40 minutes**

50 g (2 oz) butter
500 g (1 lb) parsnips, cut into
    5 mm (¼ inch) dice
500 g (1 lb) fennel bulb, cut into
    small pieces of equal size
1 onion, chopped
3 tablespoons cornflour
1.2 litres (2 pints) hot Vegetable
    or Chicken Stock (see pages 8
    and 9)
150 ml (¼ pint) double cream
salt and pepper

1 Melt the butter in a large saucepan. Add the parsnips, fennel and onion and cook over a moderate heat for 15 minutes, or until the vegetables are soft, stirring constantly.

2 In a small bowl, mix the cornflour with 150 ml (¼ pint) of the hot stock until thick and smooth. Fold the mixture into the vegetables, then pour in the remaining hot stock, stirring the soup constantly.

3 Bring the mixture to the boil, then lower the heat and simmer, partially covered, for 20 minutes, stirring frequently. Add salt and pepper to taste, stir in the cream and heat through without boiling. Serve at once in warmed soup bowls.

Carrot and ginger soup

serves **4**
preparation time **20 minutes**
cooking time **25–30 minutes**

2 tablespoons olive oil
1 large onion, chopped
1–2 garlic cloves, crushed
1 tablespoon finely grated fresh
    root ginger
375 g (12 oz) carrots, sliced
900 ml (1½ pints) Vegetable or
    Chicken Stock (see pages 8
    and 9)
2 tablespoons lime or lemon juice
salt and pepper

To serve
soured cream
2 spring onions, finely chopped

1 Heat the oil in a saucepan over a low heat, add the onion, garlic and ginger and cook for 5–6 minutes, or until softened.

2 Add the carrots and stock and bring to the boil, then reduce the heat and simmer for 15–20 minutes, or until the carrots are tender.

3 Purée the soup in a blender or food processor with the lime or lemon juice until smooth. Strain it through a sieve and return to the saucepan to reheat. Serve with a spoonful of soured cream in each bowl of soup and sprinkle with spring onions.

Potato soup with parsley

serves **4**
preparation time **10 minutes**
cooking time **20 minutes**

1.5 litres (2½ pints) Beef Stock
  (see page 11)
4 potatoes, coarsely grated
1 egg yolk
1 hard-boiled egg yolk, mashed
50 ml (2 fl oz) single cream
50 g (2 oz) grated Parmesan
  cheese
1 tablespoon finely chopped
  parsley
salt and pepper
125 g (4 oz) croûtons, to serve
  (see below)

1 Put the stock into a saucepan and bring to the boil. Sprinkle the potatoes with salt and pepper to taste, then drop them into the boiling stock. Cook for about 15 minutes, stirring from time to time.

2 Beat the egg yolk in a soup tureen and add the mashed hard-boiled egg yolk. Blend the cream, Parmesan and parsley into the egg mixture and whisk them together.

3 Carefully pour 250 ml (8 fl oz) of the stock into the egg mixture. Reheat the remaining stock and potatoes and gradually add them to the soup tureen. Sprinkle with croûtons and serve in warmed soup bowls.

tip To make croûtons, cut the crusts off 2 slices of white bread, then cube the bread. Heat 1 tablespoon vegetable oil in a heavy-based frying pan and fry the bread cubes, turning and stirring frequently, for 1–2 minutes, or until golden and crisp.

Courgette and mint soup

serves **4**
preparation time **20 minutes**
cooking time **20–25 minutes**

50 g (2 oz) butter
1 small onion, chopped
1–2 garlic cloves, crushed
750 g (1½ lb) courgettes, diced
finely grated rind of 1 lemon
600 ml (1 pint) Vegetable or
    Chicken Stock (see pages 8
    and 9), or water
2–3 tablespoons chopped mint
2 egg yolks
100 ml (3½ fl oz) double cream
salt and pepper
single cream, to garnish

1 Melt the butter in a saucepan over a low heat, add the onion and garlic and cook for 5–6 minutes, or until softened. Stir in the courgettes and lemon rind and cook for a further 5–10 minutes, or until tender. Add the stock or water and mint and bring to the boil, then lower the heat and simmer for 5 minutes.

2 Purée the soup in a blender or food processor until smooth, then strain through a sieve.

3 Immediately before serving, reheat the soup to just below boiling point. Mix together the egg yolks and double cream in a small bowl and whisk in a ladleful of the hot soup. Whisk this mixture back into the pan; do not allow the soup to boil or it will curdle. Season to taste with salt and pepper and serve in warmed soup bowls. Drizzle with single cream before serving.

Pea, lettuce and lemon soup with sesame croûtons

serves **4**
preparation time **10 minutes**
cooking time **20 minutes**

25 g (1 oz) butter
1 large onion, finely chopped
425 g (14 oz) frozen peas
2 Little Gem lettuces, roughly
    chopped
1 litre (1³/₄ pints) Vegetable or
    Chicken Stock (see pages 8
    and 9)
grated rind and juice of ¹/₂ lemon
salt and pepper

Sesame croûtons

2 thick slices of bread, cubed
1 tablespoon olive oil
1 tablespoon sesame seeds

1 To make the sesame croûtons, brush the bread cubes with the oil and place in a roasting tin. Sprinkle with the sesame seeds and cook in a preheated oven at 200°C (400°F), Gas Mark 6, for 10–15 minutes, or until golden.

2 Meanwhile, heat the butter in a large saucepan, add the onion and cook for 5 minutes, or until beginning to soften. Add the peas, lettuce, stock, lemon rind and juice and seasoning. Bring to the boil, then reduce the heat, cover and simmer for 10–15 minutes.

3 Allow the soup to cool slightly, then transfer to a blender or food processor and purée until smooth. Return the soup to the pan, adjust the seasoning if necessary and heat through. Spoon into warmed soup bowls and sprinkle with the sesame croûtons.

Spinach and broccoli soup

serves **4**
preparation time **10 minutes**
cooking time **20 minutes**

2 tablespoons olive oil
50 g (2 oz) butter
1 onion, diced
1 garlic clove, finely chopped
2 potatoes, diced
250 g (8 oz) broccoli, chopped
300 g (10 oz) spinach, chopped
900 ml (1½ pints) Vegetable or
   Chicken Stock (see pages 8
   and 9)
125 g (4 oz) Gorgonzola cheese,
   crumbled into small pieces
juice of ½ lemon
½ teaspoon grated nutmeg
salt and pepper
75 g (3 oz) toasted pine nuts,
   to garnish
warm crusty bread, to serve

1 Heat the oil and butter in a saucepan, add the onion and garlic and cook for 3 minutes. Add the potatoes, broccoli, spinach and stock and bring to the boil, then lower the heat and simmer for 15 minutes.

2 Add the Gorgonzola to the soup with the lemon juice, nutmeg and salt and pepper to taste. For a smooth consistency, purée the soup in a blender or food processor. Alternatively, it can be left with chunky pieces according to taste. Spoon into warmed soup bowls, garnish with toasted pine nuts and serve with warm crusty bread.

Watercress soup with poached quails' eggs

serves **4**
preparation time **5 minutes**
cooking time **20–25 minutes**

50 g (2 oz) butter
1 onion, finely chopped
250 g (8 oz) potatoes, cut into
   1 cm (½ inch) cubes
300 g (10 oz) watercress, roughly
   chopped
900 ml (1½ pints) Vegetable or
   Chicken Stock (see pages 8
   and 9)
300 ml (½ pint) single cream
12 quails' eggs
salt and pepper
50 g (2 oz) Parmesan cheese, finely
   grated, to serve

1 Melt the butter in a large saucepan, add the onion and cook gently, without allowing it to colour, for 8–10 minutes, or until well softened. Stir in the potatoes and watercress, cover and cook for 3–5 minutes, stirring once or twice, until the watercress has just wilted.

2 Add the stock and season with salt and pepper. Bring to the boil, then lower the heat and simmer for 6–8 minutes, or until the potatoes are tender.

3 Purée the soup in a blender or food processor until smooth. Strain it through a sieve and return to the pan. Add the cream, adjust the seasoning to taste and heat through without boiling.

4 Poach the quails' eggs in a saucepan of gently simmering water. Remove the eggs with a slotted spoon and drain well on kitchen paper. Place 3 eggs in each serving bowl. Ladle the watercress soup over the eggs and serve with the grated Parmesan.

Avgolemono

serves **4–6**
preparation time **about
10 minutes**
cooking time **25 minutes**

1.5 litres (2½ pints) Vegetable or
    Chicken Stock (see pages 8
    and 9)
50 g (2 oz) long-grain white rice
2 eggs
2–3 tablespoons lemon juice
salt and pepper
1 tablespoon chopped parsley,
    to garnish (optional)

1 Combine the stock, ½ teaspoon of salt and the rice in a saucepan. Bring the mixture to the boil. Stir, then lower the heat, cover and simmer for 20 minutes. Stir once more.

2 Beat the eggs in a small bowl, then whisk in the lemon juice. Add a ladleful of stock, beat, then add another ladleful of stock and beat again.

3 Bring the remaining stock and rice mixture to the boil. Briefly remove the saucepan from the heat and add the egg and lemon mixture. Stir well, lower the heat and simmer for a further 2 minutes, then add salt and pepper to taste. Sprinkle on the parsley, if liked. Serve immediately in warmed soup bowls.

Crab soup

serves **4–6**
preparation time **10 minutes**
cooking time **about 20 minutes**

1 litre (1³/₄ pints) Chicken Stock
  (see page 9)
2.5 cm (1 inch) piece of fresh root
  ginger, peeled and very finely
  chopped
2 ripe tomatoes, skinned, deseeded
  and very finely chopped
¹/₂ small red or green chilli,
  deseeded and very finely
  chopped
2 tablespoons rice wine or
  dry sherry
1 tablespoon rice wine vinegar or
  white wine or cider vinegar
¹/₂ teaspoon sugar
1 tablespoon cornflour
about 150 g (5 oz) white crab
  meat, defrosted and drained
  thoroughly if frozen
salt and pepper
2 spring onions, finely sliced
  lengthways, to garnish

1 Put the stock into a large saucepan with the ginger, tomatoes, chilli, rice wine or sherry, vinegar and sugar. Bring to the boil, then cover, lower the heat and simmer for about 10 minutes to allow the flavours to mingle and mellow.

2 Blend the cornflour to a paste with a little cold water, then pour it into the soup and stir to mix. Simmer, stirring, for 1–2 minutes, or until the soup thickens.

3 Add the crab meat, stir gently to mix, then heat through for 2–3 minutes. Taste and add salt and pepper if necessary. Serve piping hot in warmed soup bowls, sprinkled with the sliced spring onions.

tip Frozen white crab meat is convenient to use and it can be found in large supermarkets. Alternatively, you can buy a whole cooked fresh crab from a fishmonger and have the meat removed for you.

Chicken and coconut milk soup

serves **4**
preparation time **6 minutes**
cooking time **10 minutes**

300 ml (½ pint) Chicken Stock
   (see page 9)
3 Kaffir lime leaves, torn
½ lemon grass stalk, obliquely
   sliced
2.5 cm (1 inch) piece of galangal,
   peeled and finely sliced
100 ml (3½ fl oz) coconut milk
4 tablespoons Thai fish sauce
1 teaspoon palm sugar or light
   muscovado sugar
3 tablespoons lime juice
125 g (4 oz) chicken, skinned and
   cut into bite-sized pieces
2 tablespoons chilli oil or 2 small
   chillies, finely sliced (optional)

1 Heat the stock in a saucepan, then stir in the lime leaves, lemon grass and galangal. As the stock is simmering, add the coconut milk, fish sauce, sugar and lime juice and stir well.

2 Add the chicken and simmer for 5 minutes.

3 Just before serving, add the chilli oil or chillies, if liked, stir again and serve in warmed soup bowls.

Pork ball and tofu soup

serves **4**
preparation time **10 minutes**
cooking time **12–13 minutes**

600 ml (1 pint) Chicken Stock
   (see page 9)
1 garlic clove, finely chopped
4 garlic cloves, halved
$\frac{1}{2}$ teaspoon ground black pepper
8 fresh coriander roots
200 g (7 oz) silken tofu, cut into
   2.5 cm (1 inch) slices
1 sheet roasted laver seaweed,
   torn into shreds
2 tablespoons light soy sauce
fresh coriander leaves, to garnish

Pork balls
65 g (2$\frac{1}{2}$ oz) minced pork
1 tablespoon light soy sauce
$\frac{1}{2}$ teaspoon ground black pepper

1 Heat the stock with the chopped and halved garlic, pepper and coriander in a saucepan. While the soup is heating, make the pork balls.

2 Mix together the pork, soy sauce and pepper, then form the mixture into small balls. Drop them into the soup and simmer gently for 6–7 minutes.

3 Add the tofu, laver and soy sauce, stir for 30 seconds, then serve the soup in warmed bowls, garnished with coriander leaves.

Prawn and lemon grass soup

serves **4**
preparation time **25 minutes**
cooking time **20 minutes**

375 g (12 oz) raw prawns
3 lemon grass stalks, cut into
   2.5 cm (1 inch) pieces
1.2 litres (2 pints) water
1 tomato, quartered and deseeded
475 g (15 oz) can straw
   mushrooms, drained
6 Kaffir lime leaves
1 spring onion, chopped
185 g (6½ oz) bean sprouts
juice of 3 limes
2 small red chillies, finely sliced
4 tablespoons Vietnamese or Thai
   fish sauce
salt and pepper
fresh coriander leaves, to garnish

1 Peel and devein the prawns and set aside the shells. Cut off the white part of the lemon grass stalks, reserving the tops. Flatten the lemon grass stalks with a cleaver or pestle.

2 Heat the measured water in a saucepan and add the prawn shells and the lemon grass tops. Bring the water slowly to the boil, strain and return to the saucepan. Add the flattened lemon grass, tomato, straw mushrooms and lime leaves. Bring back to the boil, then lower the heat to a simmer and cook for 3–4 minutes.

3 Add the prawns and, when they have changed colour, add the spring onion, bean sprouts, lime juice, chillies and fish sauce. Season to taste with salt and pepper and stir well.

4 Serve in individual warmed soup bowls, sprinkled with coriander leaves.

Classic Soups

Everyone has a favourite soup and these
recipes show you how to make them with
minimum fuss. From the creamy *Vichyssoise*
and the chunky *Minestrone*, to the spicy
Mulligatawny and the luxurious *Prawn Bisque*.

Tomato soup with croûtons

serves **4**
preparation time **10 minutes**
cooking time **40 minutes**

4 tablespoons olive oil
1 onion, chopped
3 garlic cloves, crushed
750 g (1½ lb) tomatoes, skinned
   and chopped
1 litre (1¾ pints) Vegetable or
   Chicken Stock (see pages 8
   and 9)
salt and pepper
croûtons, to serve (see page 18)
a few basil leaves, chopped,
   to garnish

1 Heat half the oil in a large saucepan, add the onion and garlic and cook gently for 4–6 minutes, or until golden but not brown. Add the tomatoes and cook for 5 minutes, then gradually stir in the stock. Add salt and pepper to taste, then simmer for 30 minutes.

2 Meanwhile, make the croûtons.

3 Add the croûtons and the basil to the soup and serve immediately in warmed soup bowls.

Pumpkin soup

serves **6**

preparation time **about**

10 minutes

cooking time **40–45 minutes**

50 g (2 oz) butter

750 g (1 ½ lb) pumpkin, skinned,
  deseeded and cut into
  large pieces

150 ml (¼ pint) warm water

¼ teaspoon grated nutmeg

pinch of dried thyme

1.5 litres (2½ pints) milk

50 g (2 oz) long-grain white rice

salt and pepper

croûtons, to garnish (see page 18)

1 Melt the butter in a large saucepan. Add the pumpkin, stir well and cook over a low to moderate heat for 10 minutes. Add the measured warm water, nutmeg, thyme and salt and pepper to taste. Cover and cook over a high heat until the pumpkin is soft.

2 Purée the pumpkin mixture in a blender or food processor, with a little of the milk if necessary, until smooth. Transfer to a clean saucepan.

3 Add the remaining milk and rice to the pumpkin purée in the pan. Stir well and cook, covered, for 30 minutes, or until the rice is tender, stirring from time to time. Serve the pumpkin soup in warmed bowls, garnished with croûtons.

Roasted pepper soup with black pepper cream

serves **4**
preparation time **20 minutes**
cooking time **about 1 hour**

6 large red or yellow peppers
4 leeks, white and pale green parts
　only, thinly sliced
3 tablespoons olive oil
750 ml (1¼ pints) Vegetable or
　Chicken Stock (see pages 8
　and 9)
2 teaspoons black peppercorns
75 ml (3 fl oz) mascarpone cheese
75 ml (3 fl oz) milk
salt and pepper
toasted crusty bread, to serve

1 Put the peppers into a large roasting tin and roast in a preheated oven, 240°C (475°F), Gas Mark 9, for 20–30 minutes, turning once, until they begin to char. Remove the peppers from the oven, put them into a polythene bag and close it tightly. Leave for 10 minutes to steam.

2 Put the leeks into a bowl of cold water to soak for 5 minutes.

3 Remove the peppers from the bag and peel off the skins, then pull out the stalks – the seeds should come with them. Halve the peppers, scrape out any remaining seeds and roughly chop the flesh. Swish the leeks around in the water to loosen any mud, then drain and rinse well.

4 Heat the oil in a large saucepan, add the leeks and cook gently for 10 minutes until soft but not coloured. Add the peppers, stock and a little salt and pepper. Bring the mixture to the boil, then lower the heat and simmer for 20 minutes.

5 Pound or grind the black peppercorns as finely as possible. Beat the mascarpone with the milk and pepper. Season with salt, cover and chill in the refrigerator until needed.

6 Purée the soup in a blender or food processor, then pass it through a sieve into the rinsed-out pan. Reheat, taste and adjust the seasoning if necessary. Serve the soup in warmed bowls with dollops of the pepper cream and slices of toasted crusty bread.

Vichyssoise

serves **6**

preparation time **15 minutes**, plus chilling

cooking time **about 35–40 minutes**

50 g (2 oz) butter

1 kg (2 lb) leeks, white parts only, finely sliced

1 onion, chopped

1 litre (1¾ pints) Vegetable or Chicken Stock (see pages 8 and 9)

pinch of grated nutmeg

750 g (1½ lb) old potatoes, cubed

600 ml (1 pint) milk

300 ml (½ pint) single cream

150 ml (¼ pint) double cream, chilled

salt and white pepper

2 tablespoons snipped fresh chives, to garnish

1 Melt the butter in a saucepan. Add the leeks and onion and cook over a moderate heat for 5 minutes, stirring constantly. Do not allow the vegetables to change colour.

2 Add the stock, nutmeg, potatoes and salt and pepper to taste. Bring the mixture to the boil, then lower the heat and cook, partially covered, for 25 minutes. Pour in the milk and simmer for a further 5–8 minutes. Cool slightly.

3 Purée the mixture in a blender or food processor until smooth, then rub it through a sieve into a bowl. Add the single cream, stir well and cover the bowl closely. Chill in the refrigerator for at least 3 hours.

4 Just before serving, swirl in the double cream and add more salt and pepper if required. Serve in chilled bowls, garnishing each portion with a generous sprinkling of snipped chives.

Leek and potato soup

serves **4–6**
preparation time **15 minutes**
cooking time **40 minutes**

25 g (1 oz) butter
2 large leeks, finely sliced
250 g (8 oz) potatoes, roughly
  diced
1 onion, roughly chopped
750 ml (1¼ pints) Vegetable or
  Chicken Stock (see pages 8
  and 9), or water
300 ml (½ pint) milk
salt and pepper
1 tablespoon snipped chives,
  to garnish

1 Melt the butter in a large saucepan, add the leeks, potatoes and onion and stir well to coat with the butter. Cover tightly with a piece of greaseproof paper and cook over a very gentle heat for about 15 minutes, or until the vegetables have softened, stirring frequently to prevent them from browning.

2 Add the stock or water and milk and season to taste with salt and pepper. Bring to the boil, then lower the heat and simmer gently for about 20 minutes, or until the vegetables are tender.

3 Purée the mixture in a blender or food processor until smooth, then transfer it to a clean saucepan.

4 Adjust the seasoning if necessary and heat until very hot, then pour the soup into warmed bowls. Garnish with chives and serve.

Mushroom soup with crispy bacon

serves **4–6**
preparation time **15 minutes**
cooking time **25–30 minutes**

50 g (2 oz) butter
1 onion, finely chopped
1 clove garlic, finely chopped
375 g (12 oz) mushrooms,
    thinly sliced
2 tablespoons plain flour
600 ml (1 pint) Chicken Stock
    (see page 9)
150 ml (¼ pint) milk
1 tablespoon Manzanilla sherry
    (optional)
150 ml (¼ pint) single cream
4 rindless bacon rashers, cooked
    until crisp and broken into
    small pieces
salt and pepper
chervil sprigs, to garnish

1 Melt the butter in a large saucepan, add the onion, garlic and mushrooms and cook until soft and beginning to colour. Sprinkle on the flour and stir to combine. Gradually pour on the stock and milk, stirring well to blend. Bring to the boil, then lower the heat and simmer for about 15–20 minutes.

2 Add salt and pepper to taste, along with the sherry, if using, and half the cream. Reheat the soup without boiling, then pour into warmed soup bowls. Whip the remaining cream until it is just holding its shape, then spoon a little on top of each bowl of soup. Sprinkle with the bacon pieces and garnish with chervil sprigs.

tip A mixture of cultivated and wild mushrooms gives the soup a very special flavour. For a smoother soup, purée it before adding the cream.

French onion soup

serves **6**
preparation time **10 minutes**
cooking time **about 35 minutes**

50 g (2 oz) butter
500 g (1 lb) Spanish onions, sliced
    into fairly thick rings
25 g (1 oz) plain flour
1.2 litres (2 pints) Vegetable or
    Beef Stock (see pages 8 and 11)
1 tablespoon Cognac (optional)
½ teaspoon Dijon mustard
salt and pepper

To garnish
6 slices of French bread
75 g (3 oz) Gruyère cheese, grated
finely chopped parsley

1 Melt the butter in a large saucepan, add the onions and cook over a moderate heat, stirring constantly, until soft and pale gold in colour. Sprinkle in the flour and stir for about 1 minute, then gradually pour in the stock. Bring the mixture to the boil, stirring constantly, and add salt and pepper to taste.

2 Lower the heat and simmer for 20–25 minutes. Stir in the Cognac, if using, and the mustard. Keep the soup hot.

3 Grill the bread for the garnish until it is lightly browned, then sprinkle each slice with the grated Gruyère. Pour the soup into heatproof bowls and float a slice of cheese-topped bread in each bowl. Put the bowls under a preheated grill until the cheese melts and bubbles. Sprinkle with chopped parsley and serve the soup immediately.

Ham and pea soup

serves **6**
preparation time **10 minutes**,
plus soaking
cooking time **1¼ hours**

250 g (8 oz) yellow or green split
   peas, soaked for 4–6 hours in
   cold water to cover
50 g (2 oz) butter
1 large onion, roughly chopped
1 large carrot, roughly chopped
4 thick bacon rashers,
   approximately 175 g (6 oz),
   derinded and diced
1 small bay leaf
1 ham bone
1.2 litres (2 pints) water
2 tablespoons snipped chives
salt and pepper

1 Drain the split peas in a colander and discard the soaking water.

2 Melt the butter in a saucepan, add the onion, carrot and two-thirds of the bacon and cook gently for about 15 minutes, or until soft. Add the drained split peas, bay leaf, ham bone and measured water. Bring to the boil, then lower the heat and simmer gently for 1 hour.

3 Remove from the heat and discard the ham bone. Season with pepper and salt, if necessary. Return the saucepan to the heat. Cook the remaining bacon in a hot frying pan until crisp, then add to the soup along with half the chives. Serve the soup in warmed bowls garnished with the remaining chives.

Green lentil and bacon soup

serves **6–8**
preparation time **15–20 minutes**
cooking time **1¼ hours**

25 g (1 oz) butter
125 g (4 oz) rindless smoked lean
  bacon, finely chopped
1 garlic clove, finely chopped
1 onion, finely chopped
425 g (14 oz) green lentils, rinsed
  and drained
1 celery stick, sliced
1 large carrot, diced
1 parsley sprig
1 thyme sprig or ¼ teaspoon
  dried thyme
1 bay leaf
1.2 litres (2 pints) Chicken Stock
  (see page 9)
900 ml (1½ pints) water
1 lemon slice
salt and pepper

1 Melt the butter in a large saucepan. Add the bacon, garlic and onion and cook over a moderate to high heat for 5 minutes, stirring constantly.

2 Lower the heat and add the lentils, celery, carrot, parsley, thyme and bay leaf to the pan. Pour in the stock and the measured water. Bring the mixture to the boil, skimming off the scum as it rises to the surface with a slotted spoon. Add the lemon slice.

3 Lower the heat, cover and simmer for 55–60 minutes, stirring occasionally. If the soup is too thick, stir in a little more water. Carefully remove and discard the parsley and thyme sprigs, bay leaf and lemon slice. Add salt and pepper to taste if necessary.

4 Measure 600 ml (1 pint) of the soup and purée it in a blender or food processor until smooth. Return the purée to the soup, stir well and cook over a moderate heat for 5 minutes. Serve in warmed soup bowls.

Turkey and vegetable soup

serves **8**
preparation time **25 minutes**
cooking time **about 2 hours**

1 large turkey drumstick, about
  750 g (1½ lb)
2.4 litres (4 pints) water
1 small unpeeled onion, studded
  with 4 cloves plus 1 large onion,
  peeled and chopped
2 sprigs of parsley
1 bouquet garni
1 teaspoon salt
1 sprig of thyme, or ¼ teaspoon
  dried thyme
1 sprig of marjoram, or ½ teaspoon
  dried marjoram
3 carrots, chopped
2 celery sticks, sliced
250 g (8 oz) red lentils rinsed and
  drained
250 g (8 oz) potatoes, peeled and
  cut into 1 cm (½ inch) cubes
3 leeks, sliced
3 turnips, peeled and cut into 1 cm
  (½ inch) cubes
2 tablespoons light soy sauce
pepper
3–4 tablespoons finely chopped
  fresh parsley, to garnish

1 Place the drumstick in a large saucepan. Add the measured water, the studded onion, parsley sprigs, bouquet garni, salt, thyme and marjoram. Bring the mixture to the boil, lower the heat and simmer, partially covered, for 45 minutes.

2 Add the chopped onion, carrots and celery. Cook for 30 minutes over a low to moderate heat, then add the lentils, potatoes, leeks and turnips. Cook, until all the vegetables are tender. Remove the drumstick and let it cool. Remove and discard the bouquet garni, the studded onion with cloves and any parsley, thyme or marjoram stems.

3 Cut the turkey meat off the bone, discarding the skin. Carefully remove any small bones. Cut the meat into small pieces and return it to the saucepan. Add the soy sauce to the pan with pepper to taste. Heat the soup thoroughly and serve in a soup tureen, garnished with the parsley.

Cream of chicken soup

serves **6**
preparation time **15 minutes**
cooking time **1¼ hours**

1 chicken carcass
1 onion
1 bouquet garni
1 litre (2 pints) Chicken Stock
  (see page 9)
125 g (4 oz) cooked chicken
300 ml (½ pint) milk
50 g (2 oz) plain flour
2 tablespoons water
1 tablespoon lemon juice
¼ teaspoon grated nutmeg
salt and pepper

To garnish
croûtons (see page 18)
flat leaf parsley sprigs
grated nutmeg

To serve
150 ml (¼ pint) single cream
lemon wedges

1 Put the carcass, onion and bouquet garni into a saucepan with the stock. Simmer for about 1 hour. Strain the liquid and return it to the saucepan.

2 Neatly dice the cooked chicken meat and add to the stock with the milk. Blend the flour with the measured water, then slowly add the mixture to the stock, stirring constantly. Bring to the boil, then lower the heat and simmer gently for 10 minutes. Season the soup with lemon juice, nutmeg and salt and pepper to taste.

3 Pour the soup into warmed soup bowls, pour over the cream and garnish with croûtons, flat leaf parsley sprigs and some grated nutmeg. Serve with lemon wedges on the side.

Minestrone

serves **8–10**

preparation time **about 30 minutes**, plus soaking

cooking time **about 2¾ hours**

250 g (8 oz) dried haricot beans, soaked overnight in cold water to cover

3 tablespoons olive oil

2 onions, finely chopped

2 garlic cloves, finely chopped

2 rindless streaky bacon rashers, finely chopped

6 tomatoes, skinned and chopped

1.8 litres (3 pints) water

600 ml (1 pint) Beef Stock (see page 11)

1 courgette, diced

1 tablespoon chopped fresh marjoram or 1 teaspoon dried marjoram

1 teaspoon chopped fresh thyme or ½ teaspoon dried thyme

2 tablespoons tomato purée

2 carrots, diced

2 celery sticks, finely sliced

½ Savoy cabbage, finely shredded

250 g (8 oz) fresh shelled or frozen peas

50 g (2 oz) dried spaghetti, broken into small pieces or small pasta shapes

1 tablespoon chopped parsley

150 g (5 oz) grated Parmesan cheese

salt and pepper

1 Drain the beans thoroughly in a colander, then rinse under cold running water and drain again.

2 Heat the oil in a large saucepan, add the onions, garlic and bacon and cook over a moderate heat until the onions are transparent, but not brown, and the bacon is crisp.

3 Stir in the tomatoes, the measured water and stock, then add the courgette, beans, marjoram, thyme and tomato purée. Bring the mixture to the boil, skimming off the scum as it rises to the surface with a slotted spoon. Lower the heat and simmer, covered, for about 2 hours, or until the beans are tender.

4 Add the carrots and celery and cook over a moderate heat for a further 15 minutes, then add the cabbage, peas and pasta. Cook for 15–18 minutes, or until the vegetables and pasta are tender.

5 Add a little more water if the soup is too thick. Add the parsley, season to taste with salt and pepper and stir in 50 g (2 oz) of the Parmesan. Serve the soup immediately in warmed bowls, with the remaining Parmesan served separately.

Mulligatawny

serves **6–8**
preparation time **15–20 minutes**
cooking time **30–35 minutes**

1 onion, chopped
2 garlic cloves, chopped
2.5 cm (1 inch) piece of fresh root
  ginger, peeled and chopped
¼ teaspoon cayenne pepper
1 teaspoon ground coriander
½ teaspoon ground cumin
1 teaspoon ground turmeric
4 teaspoons vegetable oil
3 boneless, skinless chicken
  breasts, halved
1.2 litres (2 pints) Chicken Stock
  (see page 9)
1.2 litres (2 pints) water
50 g (2 oz) long-grain white rice
125 g (4 oz) red lentils
1 tablespoon lemon juice
2 tablespoons grated creamed
  coconut
salt
6–8 lemon slices, to garnish

1 In a blender or food processor, purée the onion, garlic and ginger with the cayenne, coriander, cumin and turmeric to a smooth paste, scraping down the sides of the jug or bowl with a wooden or plastic spatula from time to time.

2 Heat the oil in a large saucepan and cook the onion paste over a moderate heat, stirring, for 2–3 minutes. Add the chicken breasts and cook, stirring, for a further 1–2 minutes.

3 Slowly pour in the stock and measured water, stirring constantly. Add the rice and lentils and simmer for 15–20 minutes, or until the rice is tender.

4 Remove the chicken, cut it into small pieces and set aside. Purée 900 ml (1½ pints) of the soup mixture in a blender or food processor, then return it to the remaining soup in the pan. Add a little water if the soup is too thick and salt to taste.

5 Stir well, then add the lemon juice, coconut and reserved chicken pieces. Stir again and heat thoroughly without boiling for 3–5 minutes. Serve in warmed soup bowls, garnishing each portion with a lemon slice.

Bouillabaisse

serves **6–8**

preparation time **about**

35 minutes

cooking time **35–40 minutes**

4 tablespoons olive oil

2 garlic cloves, finely chopped

2 onions, chopped

500 g (1 lb) prepared mackerel,
cut into chunks

500 g (1 lb) whiting fillet,
cut into chunks

500 g (1 lb) haddock or cod fillet,
cut into chunks

250 g (8 oz) raw prawns, peeled

6 tomatoes, skinned and chopped

½ teaspoon saffron threads

1.5 litres (2½ pints) hot Fish Stock
(see page 10)

1 bay leaf

3 parsley sprigs

10–12 live mussels, scrubbed and
debearded

6–8 slices of French bread

salt and pepper

2 tablespoons finely chopped
parsley, to garnish

1 Heat the oil in a large saucepan. Add the garlic and onions and cook, covered, for 3–5 minutes, or until the onions are transparent but not brown. Add the mackerel, whiting and haddock or cod and cook, uncovered, over a moderate heat for 10 minutes. Stir from time to time.

2 Add the prawns and tomatoes. Dissolve the saffron threads in the hot stock and add to the pan with the bay leaf, parsley sprigs and salt and pepper to taste. Stir and bring the mixture to the boil. Lower the heat and simmer, covered, for 15 minutes, then add the mussels and continue cooking for a further 10 minutes, or until the fish is cooked.

3 Remove and discard the bay leaf and parsley sprigs and any mussels that have not opened. Put the bread into a warmed soup tureen and ladle in the soup. Sprinkle with the chopped parsley before serving.

Clam chowder

serves **6–8**
preparation time **25–45 minutes**
cooking time **35–40 minutes**

48–60 live clams in closed shells
  (discard any that do not shut
  immediately when sharply
  tapped)
40 g (1½ oz) butter
125 g (4 oz) smoked streaky bacon,
  derinded and diced
2 large onions, finely chopped
2 celery sticks, diced
1–2 leeks, sliced
2 tablespoons finely chopped
  parsley, plus extra to garnish
2 bay leaves
leaves from 1 thyme sprig
900 ml (1½ pints) water
ground nutmeg
4–5 medium potatoes, diced
2 tablespoons plain flour
1–2 teaspoons, Worcestershire
  sauce
finely ground sea salt (optional)
  and pepper

1 Put the clams on a baking sheet in a preheated oven, 200°C (400°F), Gas Mark 6, for 2–3 minutes, or until they open slightly, then remove them and prise the shells apart. Open the shells over a bowl to catch all the clam juice. Snip off the inedible black-tipped necks (which resemble a tube), roughly chop the coral-coloured and pink flesh and leave the softer body meat whole.

2 Melt 25 g (1 oz) of the butter in a large saucepan. Add the bacon and cook for about 5 minutes, or until the fat starts to run. Add the onions, cover and cook gently for 10 minutes. Add the celery, leeks, parsley, bay leaves and thyme and cook for a further 5 minutes. Add the reserved clam juice, the measured water, nutmeg and pepper to taste and the potatoes. Stir well, taste and season with salt if necessary. Simmer gently for about 10 minutes, or until the potatoes are almost tender.

3 Meanwhile, cream the flour with the remaining butter to a smooth paste and reserve. Add the clams to the pan and simmer very gently for 3–4 minutes. Do not boil the soup or the clams will be tough and rubbery. Add a piece of the butter and flour paste to the pan, stirring well. When it has been fully incorporated, stir in a little more and continue until all the paste has been added. Stir for another 3–4 minutes, or until the soup thickens slightly.

4 Increase the heat briefly for 10 seconds, then remove from the heat. Add the Worcestershire sauce, stir and serve immediately in warmed soup bowls, garnished with parsley.

Prawn bisque

serves **4**
preparation time **20 minutes**
cooking time **35–45 minutes**

50 g (2 oz) butter
1 small carrot, finely chopped
½ small onion, finely chopped
½ celery stick, finely chopped
500 g (1 lb) raw prawns in their
 shells
250 ml (8 fl oz) dry white wine
2 tablespoons brandy
1.2 litres (2 pints) Fish Stock
 (see page 10)
1 bouquet garni
25 g (1 oz) long-grain white rice
100 ml (3½ fl oz) double cream
pinch of cayenne pepper
salt and pepper
4 tablespoons chopped parsley,
 to garnish

1 Melt the butter in a large heavy-based saucepan, add the carrot, onion and celery and cook, stirring occasionally, for 8–10 minutes, or until softened and lightly golden. Increase the heat, add the prawns and cook for 3–4 minutes, or until the shells turn pink all over.

2 Add the wine and brandy and bring to the boil, then lower the heat and simmer for 3–4 minutes, or until the prawns are cooked. Remove the prawns and leave to cool slightly. When cool enough to handle, peel the prawns, reserving the shells. Remove the black veins running down the back, chop the flesh and set aside.

3 Bring the liquid back to the boil and boil rapidly for 2–3 minutes, or until reduced by one-third. Add the reserved prawn shells with the stock, bouquet garni and rice. Bring to the boil, then lower the heat and simmer gently for 15–20 minutes, or until the rice is tender.

4 Remove and discard the bouquet garni. Purée the soup, including the shells, in a blender or food processor with three-quarters of the prawn meat. Strain through a fine sieve into a clean pan, pressing with the back of a ladle to push through as much liquid as you can. Add the cream and cayenne and season to taste with salt and pepper.

5 Bring the soup back to the boil, then lower the heat, add the reserved chopped prawns and cook for 1–2 minutes, or until heated through. Serve in warmed soup bowls, sprinkled with the chopped parsley.

Summer Soups

Whether warm or chilled, soup can be surprisingly refreshing on a hot summer's day. Packed with Mediterranean flavours, light ingredients and fragrant herbs, these elegant dishes are guaranteed to impress.

Chicory soup

serves **4**
preparation time **5 minutes**
cooking time **about 40 minutes**

75 g (3 oz) butter
1 onion, diced
2 chicory heads, finely chopped
50 ml (2 fl oz) dry white wine
1 litre (1¾ pints) milk
250 ml (8 fl oz) Vegetable or
    Chicken Stock (see pages 8
    and 9)
2 tablespoons cornflour
2 tablespoons grated Parmesan
    cheese
8 slices of stale bread, buttered
salt and pepper

1 Heat 50 g (2 oz) of the butter in a saucepan over a low heat, add the onion and cook until golden. Add the chicory and cook slowly in the butter for 10 minutes, then season to taste with salt and pepper. Pour in the wine, and when this has evaporated, stir in most of the milk and the stock. Bring slowly to the boil. Mix the cornflour with the remaining milk and add to the pan, stirring constantly to avoid lumps.

2 Cook for 25 minutes over a moderate heat, then whisk in the grated Parmesan and the remaining butter, cut into pieces.

3 Meanwhile, toast the stale bread in a preheated oven, 200°C (400°F), Gas Mark 6, for about 10 minutes, or until golden brown. Put the toast into warmed soup bowls and pour the soup over. Serve hot.

Celery, carrot and apple soup

serves **6**
preparation time **15 minutes**
cooking time **about 1 hour**

50 g (2 oz) unsalted butter
500 g (1 lb) celery, sliced
500 g (1 lb) carrots, chopped
250 g (8 oz) dessert apples, peeled,
    cored and roughly chopped
1.2 litres (2 pints) Vegetable Stock
    (see page 8)
1 teaspoon paprika
cayenne pepper, to taste
1 tablespoon chopped fresh basil
    leaves or 1 teaspoon dried basil
1 bay leaf
1 teaspoon freshly grated root
    ginger
salt and ground white pepper

To garnish
chopped celery leaves
paprika

1 Melt the butter in a large saucepan and add the celery, carrots and apple. Cover with a tight-fitting lid and cook over a low heat for 15 minutes, stirring occasionally.

2 Add the stock, paprika, cayenne, basil, bay leaf and ginger. Bring to the boil, then lower the heat and simmer, partially covered, for 40–45 minutes, or until the vegetables and apple are very soft.

3 Purée the mixture in a blender or food processor until smooth. Strain it through a sieve back into the pan and season to taste with salt and pepper. Reheat the soup. Serve the soup in warmed bowls, garnishing each portion with a few chopped celery leaves and a light sprinkling of paprika.

Jerusalem artichoke soup with artichoke crisps

serves **4**
preparation time **25 minutes**
cooking time **30 minutes**

1 small lemon
625 g (1¼ lb) Jerusalem artichokes
50 g (2 oz) butter
1 onion, chopped
1 garlic clove, crushed
1 celery stick, chopped
leaves from 1 lemon thyme sprig
1 litre (1¾ pints) Vegetable or
    Chicken Stock (see pages 8
    and 9)
vegetable oil, for deep-frying
175 ml (6 fl oz) single cream
    or milk
3 tablespoons finely grated
    Parmesan cheese
salt and pepper
flat leaf parsley leaves, to garnish

1 Finely grate the rind from the lemon and set it aside. Squeeze the juice and put it into a large bowl of cold water. Carefully peel the artichokes; reserve 2 and chop the rest into 1.5 cm (¾ inch) pieces, dropping them into the lemon water as you prepare them to prevent discoloration.

2 Melt the butter in a large saucepan, add the onion, garlic, celery, thyme and reserved lemon rind and cook gently, without allowing them to colour, for 6–8 minutes, or until softened. Drain the chopped artichokes and add to the pan with the stock. Season to taste with salt and pepper and bring to the boil. Lower the heat and simmer for about 15 minutes, or until the artichokes are tender.

3 To prepare the artichoke crisps, drain the 2 reserved whole artichokes, slice them thinly and dry well on kitchen paper. Heat some oil in a deep saucepan to 180–190°C (350–375°F), or until a cube of bread browns in 30 seconds. Add the artichoke slices in batches and fry until crisp and golden. Drain well on kitchen paper.

4 Purée the soup in a blender or food processor until smooth. Strain the soup through a sieve and return to the pan. Add the cream or milk, and a little water if too thick, season to taste and bring back to the boil. Stir in the finely grated Parmesan and serve in warmed bowls, sprinkled with the artichoke crisps and garnished with flat leaf parsley leaves.

Heart of artichoke soup with dill

serves **4–6**
preparation time **15–20 minutes**
cooking time **about 35 minutes**

50 g (2 oz) butter
1 onion, chopped
1 garlic clove, chopped
1 celery stick, sliced
425 g (14 oz) can artichoke hearts,
   drained
1.2 litres (2 pints) Vegetable or
   Chicken Stock (see pages 8
   and 9)
1 tablespoon lemon juice
3 tablespoons chopped dill
2 tablespoons plain flour
150 ml ($^1/_4$ pint) single cream
salt and ground white pepper
4–6 dill sprigs, to garnish

1 Melt the butter in a saucepan. Add the onion, garlic and celery and cook, covered, over a moderate heat for 10–12 minutes, or until all the vegetables are soft. Stir from time to time.

2 Add the artichoke hearts, replace the lid and cook for about a further 3 minutes. Pour in 1 litre ($1^3/_4$ pints) of the stock and the lemon juice. Stir in 1 tablespoon of the dill, then cook, covered, over a moderate heat for 15 minutes.

3 Purée the mixture in a blender or food processor until smooth. Transfer to a clean saucepan.

4 Mix the flour with the remaining stock in a small bowl, adding a little water if necessary. Reheat the soup, whisk in the flour mixture and stir until the soup thickens slightly. Add the remaining dill, season to taste with salt and pepper, then add the cream. Heat thoroughly but do not allow the soup to boil or it will curdle. Serve in warmed soup bowls, garnished with dill sprigs.

Cream of sweetcorn soup

serves **4–6**
preparation time **5–10 minutes**
cooking time **about 30 minutes**

40 g (1½ oz) butter
1 onion, chopped
2 potatoes, diced
25 g (1 oz) plain flour
900 ml (1½ pints) milk
1 bay leaf
2 x 350 g (11½ oz) cans
   sweetcorn, drained
2 tablespoons double cream
salt and freshly ground
   white pepper
crumbled fried bacon, to garnish
garlic croûtons, to serve
   (see page 107)

1 Melt the butter in a large saucepan, add the onion and cook over a low heat, stirring frequently, for 5 minutes without browning. Add the potatoes and cook for a further 2 minutes.

2 Stir in the flour, then gradually add the milk, stirring constantly. Bring to the boil, add the bay leaf and season to taste with salt and pepper. Add half the sweetcorn, cover and simmer for 15–20 minutes.

3 Remove and discard the bay leaf and set the soup aside to cool slightly. Purée it in a blender or food processor until smooth. Return to the pan, add the remaining sweetcorn and heat through.

4 Stir in the cream, sprinkle over the bacon and serve the soup in warmed bowls with the garlic croûtons.

Fennel and lemon soup
with black olive gremolata

serves **4**
preparation time **20 minutes**
cooking time **about 40 minutes**

75 ml (3 fl oz) olive oil
3 fat salad onions, chopped
250 g (8 oz) fennel, trimmed, cored
   and thinly sliced (reserve any
   green fronds for the gremolata)
1 potato, diced
finely grated rind and juice of
   1 lemon
750 ml (1¼ pints) Vegetable or
   Chicken Stock (see pages 8
   and 9)
salt and pepper

Black olive gremolata
1 small garlic clove, finely chopped
finely grated rind of 1 lemon
4 tablespoons chopped parsley
finely chopped green fronds from
   the fennel
16 Greek-style black olives, pitted
   and chopped

1 Heat the oil in a large saucepan, add the onions and cook for 5–10 minutes, or until beginning to soften. Add the fennel, potato and lemon rind and cook for 5 minutes. Pour in the stock and bring to the boil. Lower the heat, cover and simmer for about 25 minutes, or until the vegetables are tender.

2 Meanwhile, to make the gremolata, mix together the garlic, lemon rind, parsley and fennel fronds, then stir in the olives. Cover and chill in the refrigerator.

3 Purée the soup in a blender or food processor and pass it through a sieve to remove any strings of fennel. The soup should not be too thick, so add more stock if necessary. Return it to the rinsed-out pan. Taste and season well with salt, pepper and plenty of lemon juice. Pour into warmed soup bowls and sprinkle each serving with a portion of the gremolata, to be stirred in before eating.

Mint, cucumber and green pea soup

serves **6**

preparation time **15 minutes**,
plus chilling (if serving cold)

cooking time **25–30 minutes**

50 g (2 oz) butter

500 g (1 lb) cucumbers, peeled,
    deseeded and cut into 1 cm
    ($\frac{1}{2}$ inch) pieces

250 g (8 oz) shelled fresh or
    frozen peas

pinch of sugar

$\frac{1}{4}$ teaspoon white pepper

3 tablespoons finely chopped mint

1.2 litres (2 pints) Vegetable or
    Chicken Stock (see pages 8
    and 9)

175 g (6 oz) potatoes, roughly
    chopped

150 ml ($\frac{1}{4}$ pint) double cream
    (chilled, if the soup is to be
    served cold)

salt

1 Melt the butter in a large saucepan, add the cucumbers and cook over a moderate heat for 5 minutes, stirring occasionally. Add the peas, sugar, pepper and 2 tablespoons of the mint. Pour in the stock. Bring the mixture to the boil, then add the potatoes. Lower the heat and simmer, partially covered, for about 20 minutes, or until the potatoes are tender.

2 Purée the mixture in a blender or food processor until smooth. Transfer to a clean saucepan or, if the soup is to be served cold, to a bowl. Season to taste with salt.

3 If the soup is to be served hot, add the cream and reheat it gently without boiling. Serve in warmed bowls, garnishing each portion with a little of the remaining chopped mint. If the soup is to be served cold, cover the bowl closely and refrigerate for at least 3 hours. Just before serving, fold in the chilled cream. Serve in chilled bowls, garnished with the remaining chopped mint.

Roasted aubergine soup

serves **4–6**
preparation time **15 minutes**
cooking time **40–45 minutes**

1 kg (2 lb) aubergines
3 tablespoons olive oil
1 red onion
2 garlic cloves, crushed
1.2 litres (2 pints) Vegetable or
  Chicken Stock (see pages 8
  and 9)
200 ml (7 fl oz) crème fraîche or
  Greek yogurt
2 tablespoons chopped mint
salt and pepper
mint sprigs, to garnish

1 Put the aubergines under a preheated hot grill for about 20 minutes, turning occasionally, until the skin is well charred and the flesh has softened. Leave to cool slightly, then cut in half, scoop out the flesh and chop.

2 Heat the oil in a saucepan over a low heat, add the onion and garlic and cook gently, without colouring, for 5–6 minutes, or until softened. Add the chopped aubergine and the stock and cook for a further 10–15 minutes.

3 Purée the soup in a blender or food processor. Strain through a sieve and return to the pan to reheat. Season to taste with salt and pepper.

4 Mix the crème fraîche or Greek yogurt with the chopped mint and season to taste. Serve the soup in warmed bowls with a spoonful of the minted cream and garnish each serving with mint sprigs.

Bortsch

serves **6**
preparation time **15 minutes**
cooking time **about 1½ hours**

4 raw beetroot
4 tomatoes, skinned and chopped
1.2 litres (2 pints) Vegetable or
  Beef Stock (see pages 8 and 11)
3 large cabbage leaves, coarsely
  shredded
1 bay leaf
½ teaspoon caraway seeds
6 black peppercorns, crushed
5 tablespoons red wine vinegar
2 tablespoons sugar
6 small potatoes
salt
6 teaspoons soured cream,
  to garnish

1 Put the beetroot into a saucepan, cover with plenty of cold water and add 1 tablespoon salt. Bring to the boil, then lower the heat, cover and simmer for 35–45 minutes. Drain, discarding the liquid, then rinse the beetroot under cold water, dry with kitchen paper and slip off the skins.

2 Grate the beetroot into a large saucepan. Add the tomatoes, stock, cabbage leaves, bay leaf, caraway seeds, peppercorns, vinegar, sugar and 2 teaspoons salt. Stir well. Bring the mixture to the boil, then lower the heat, cover and simmer gently for about 30 minutes.

3 Remove and discard the bay leaf. Drop the potatoes into the soup and continue simmering until the potatoes are tender but not too soft. Serve the soup hot in warmed bowls, garnishing each portion with a teaspoon of soured cream.

Caldo verde

serves **6**
preparation time **15 minutes**
cooking time **40 minutes**

2 tablespoons olive oil
1 large onion, chopped
2 garlic cloves, chopped
500 g (1 lb) potatoes, cut into
  2.5 cm (1 inch) cubes
1.2 litres (2 pints) water or
  Vegetable Stock (see page 8)
250 g (8 oz) spring greens, finely
  shredded
2 tablespoons chopped parsley
salt and pepper
croûtons, to serve (see page 18),
  made with strips of bread
  instead of cubes

1 Heat the oil in a large frying pan, add the onion and cook for 5 minutes, or until softened but not brown. Add the garlic and potatoes and cook for a few minutes, stirring occasionally.

2 Transfer the vegetables to a large saucepan. Add the water or stock, season to taste with salt and pepper and cook for 15 minutes until the potatoes are tender.

3 Mash the potatoes roughly in their liquid, then add the spring greens and boil, uncovered, for 10 minutes.

4 Add the parsley and simmer for 2–3 minutes, or until heated through. Serve the soup in warmed bowls with croûtons.

Gazpacho

serves **6**
preparation time **10–15 minutes**,
plus chilling

2 garlic cloves, roughly chopped
¼ teaspoon salt
3 thick slices of white bread,
 crusts removed
1 kg (2 lb) tomatoes, skinned and
 roughly chopped
2 onions, roughly chopped
½ large cucumber, peeled,
 deseeded and roughly chopped
2 large green peppers, cored,
 deseeded and roughly chopped
5 tablespoons olive oil
4 tablespoons white wine vinegar
1 litre (1¾ pints) water
freshly ground black pepper

1 Combine the garlic and salt in a mortar and pound with a pestle until it is smooth. Put the bread into a bowl and cover it with cold water. Soak for 5 seconds, then drain the bread, squeezing out the moisture.

2 Set aside a quarter of the tomatoes, onions, cucumber and green peppers for the garnish. Put the remaining vegetables into a blender or food processor. Add the garlic paste, bread and oil and purée the mixture until smooth.

3 Pour the mixture into a bowl and stir in the vinegar and the measured water with pepper to taste. Cover closely and chill in the refrigerator for at least 3 hours.

4 Chop the reserved vegetables very finely and serve them separately in small bowls with the soup. Serve the soup very cold in chilled bowls.

Iced tomato and pepper soup with salsa verde

serves **4–6**
preparation time **about 30 minutes**, plus chilling

1 kg (2 lb) vine-ripened tomatoes, cored
2 large red peppers, cored, deseeded and roughly chopped
2 garlic cloves, chopped
1 small red chilli, deseeded and finely chopped
600 ml (1 pint) Mediterranean tomato juice or passata (sieved tomatoes)
6 tablespoons olive oil
2 tablespoons balsamic vinegar
salt and pepper
600 ml (1 pint) crushed ice, to serve

Salsa verde
2 garlic cloves, finely chopped
4 anchovy fillets in oil, rinsed and chopped
3 tablespoons each chopped parsley, mint and basil
2 tablespoons salted capers, rinsed and chopped
150 ml (¼ pint) olive oil, plus extra to seal
2 tablespoons lemon juice

1 Plunge the tomatoes into boiling water for 5–10 seconds, then remove them and refresh in cold water. Slip off the skins. Cut them in half around the middle and gently squeeze out and discard the seeds. Put the tomatoes into a blender or food processor.

2 Add the red peppers to the tomatoes with the garlic and chilli and blend to a rough purée. Transfer to a bowl and stir in the tomato juice or passata, oil and balsamic vinegar. Season with salt and pepper to taste, then cover and chill overnight in the refrigerator.

3 To make the salsa verde, pound 1 teaspoon salt with the garlic until creamy, using a pestle and mortar. Tip it into a bowl and stir in the anchovies, herbs, capers, oil, lemon juice and pepper to taste.

4 Stir the crushed ice into the soup and serve with the salsa verde in a separate bowl to stir into the soup.

Steamboat soup

serves **4–6**
preparation time **about**
40 minutes
cooking time **about 10 minutes**

8 tablespoons vegetable oil
10 garlic cloves, thinly sliced
1 tablespoon tamarind pulp
150 ml (¼ pint) boiling water
1.2 litres (2 pints) water
2 tablespoons Thai fish sauce
1 teaspoon caster sugar
1 small pineapple, peeled, cored
   and cut into chunks
175 g (6 oz) tomatoes, quartered
8 spring onions, finely sliced
250 g (8 oz) raw tiger prawns
3 squid, cleaned and cut into
   thick rings
250 g (8 oz) rainbow trout fillets,
   cut into pieces

To serve
handful of fresh coriander leaves
handful of basil leaves
2 large chillies, diagonally sliced

1 Heat the oil in a small saucepan and when it is hot deep-fry the garlic, a few slices at a time, until golden brown. Remove the garlic and drain on kitchen paper.

2 Put the tamarind pulp into a bowl with the measured boiling water and set aside for 20 minutes to soften and dissolve. Strain the liquid through a sieve (discarding the pods and tamarind stones) and put into a saucepan with the measured water, fish sauce, sugar, pineapple, tomatoes and spring onions. Slowly bring to the boil.

3 If you are using a steamboat, pour the flavoured stock into the hot pan containing smoking coals and add the tiger prawns, squid rings and pieces of fish. Simmer gently for 6–8 minutes. Alternatively, pour the hot stock into a large heavy-based saucepan, add the seafood and fish and simmer gently for 6–8 minutes, or until cooked and tender.

4 Serve the steamboat while the fish is still cooking, topped with coriander and basil leaves, slices of chilli and the deep-fried garlic.

Miso soup with tofu

serves **4**
preparation time **10 minutes**
cooking time **35–40 minutes**

2 tablespoons red or white miso
1 small leek, cut into fine julienne
    strips
125 g (4 oz) firm tofu, cut into
    small squares
1 tablespoon wakame seaweed

Dashi stock
15 g (½ oz) kombu seaweed
1.8 litres (3 pints) water
2 tablespoons dried tuna
    (bonito) flakes
chives, to serve

1 First make the dashi stock. Wipe the kombu seaweed with a damp cloth and put it into a saucepan with the measured water. Bring to a simmer, skimming off any scum that rises to the surface with a slotted spoon. When the soup is clear, add 1½ tablespoons of the dried tuna flakes and simmer, uncovered, for 20 minutes. Remove the pan from the heat and add the remaining dried tuna flakes. Set aside for 5 minutes, then strain the dashi and return it to the pan.

2 Mix the miso with a little of the warm stock, then add 1 tablespoon at a time to the stock, stirring all the time until the miso has dissolved. Remove from the heat until ready to serve.

3 Warm the miso soup and add the leek and tofu with the wakame seaweed.

4 To serve, blanch the chives, tie them into a bundle and float them on the top of the soup, then serve immediately in warmed bowls.

Mussel soup with saffron, basil and spinach

serves **4**
preparation time **30 minutes**
cooking time **about 20 minutes**

pinch of saffron threads
125 ml (4 fl oz) boiling water
750 g (1½ lb) live mussels,
  scrubbed and debearded
175 ml (6 fl oz) dry white wine
2 tablespoons olive oil
2 shallots, finely chopped
1 garlic clove, finely chopped
200 ml (7 fl oz) double cream
175 g (6 oz) young leaf spinach,
  trimmed
15 basil leaves, shredded

1 Put the saffron into a small heatproof bowl, pour over the measured boiling water and set aside to infuse. Discard any mussels that are broken or open. Put a large colander over another bowl.

2 Pour the wine into a saucepan large enough to accommodate all the mussels. Bring the wine to the boil and add the mussels. Cover with a tight-fitting lid and cook, shaking the pan frequently, for 2–3 minutes, or until the mussels have opened.

3 Tip the mussels into the colander and remove from their shells, discarding any that have not opened. Strain the mussel liquid through a muslin-lined sieve and set aside.

4 Heat the oil in a saucepan over a low heat, add the shallots and garlic and cook gently, without colouring, for 5–6 minutes, or until softened. Add the strained mussel liquid, cream and saffron and its infused liquid and bring to the boil. Lower the heat and add the spinach, half the basil and all the mussels. Simmer for 2 minutes, then remove from the heat, stir in the remaining basil and serve in warmed soup bowls.

Mediterranean salmon soup with rouille

serves **6**
preparation time **25 minutes**
cooking time **30 minutes**

1 tablespoon olive oil
25 g (1 oz) butter
1 onion, finely chopped
1 carrot, finely diced
1 potato, no more than 200 g
  (7 oz), diced
1 garlic clove, finely chopped
1 teaspoon paprika, plus extra
  to garnish
2 large pinches of saffron threads
2 tomatoes, skinned and diced
1 tablespoon tomato purée
900 ml (1½ pints) Fish Stock
  (see page 10)
125 ml (4 fl oz) dry white wine
2 salmon steaks, about 200 g
  (7 oz) each
150 ml (¼ pint) milk
150 ml (¼ pint) single cream
salt and pepper

Rouille
1 large mild red chilli, deseeded
  and chopped
1 garlic clove, finely chopped
3 tablespoons mayonnaise
1 small baguette, cut into 12 slices
  and toasted

1 Heat the oil and butter in a large saucepan, add the onion and cook gently for 5 minutes, stirring occasionally, until softened. Add the carrot and potato and cook for 5 minutes.

2 Stir in the garlic, paprika, saffron and tomatoes and cook for 1 minute. Add the tomato purée, stock and wine. Lower the salmon steaks into the stock and season generously with salt and pepper. Bring the stock to the boil, then lower the heat, cover and simmer for 10–12 minutes, or until the salmon flakes easily when pressed lightly with a knife.

3 Lift the salmon out of the pan, flake it into pieces using a knife and fork and discard the skin and bones. Reserve one quarter of the salmon for garnish, then return the rest to the pan and stir in the milk and cream. Purée the soup in a blender or food processor until smooth. Taste and adjust the seasoning if needed and reheat without boiling.

4 To make the rouille, purée the chilli, garlic and mayonnaise with a little salt and pepper in a blender or food processor until smooth. Toast the bread lightly on both sides and top with tiny spoonfuls of rouille. Ladle the soup into warmed bowls, sprinkle in the reserved salmon flakes and float the toasts on top. Sprinkle with paprika and serve immediately.

Lobster and sweetcorn chowder

serves **4**

preparation time **20 minutes**, plus preparing the lobsters

cooking time **1 hour**

2 cooked lobsters, 750 g
  (1½ lb) each
25 g (1 oz) butter
1 onion, finely chopped
1 carrot, finely chopped
1 celery stick, finely chopped
1 thyme sprig
1 parsley sprig
2 bay leaves
1 litre (1¾ pints) water

Chowder

200 g (7 oz) can sweetcorn,
  drained
25 g (1 oz) butter
1 small onion, chopped
1 small garlic clove, crushed
50 g (2 oz) pancetta, cut into
  small strips
300 ml (½ pint) milk
300 ml (½ pint) single cream
1 kg (2 lb) potatoes, cut into
  1.5 cm (¾ inch) dice
cayenne pepper
4 tomatoes, skinned, deseeded
  and chopped
salt and pepper

1 Cut the lobsters in half lengthways and remove and discard the greyish-green tomalley (the liver), the gills and the intestinal vein running along the back. Smash the claws and remove the meat. Cut up the remaining meat. Put the shells into a polythene bag and smash into small pieces with a rolling pin.

2 Put the butter into a large saucepan and melt over a low heat. Add the onion, carrot and celery and cook for 8–10 minutes, or until soft.

3 Add the herbs, measured water and pieces of lobster shell. Bring to the boil, then lower the heat and simmer for 30 minutes. Strain through a fine sieve.

4 To make the chowder, place two-thirds of the sweetcorn in a blender or food processor with the strained lobster broth and purée until smooth. Melt the butter in a large flameproof casserole, add the onion and garlic and cook gently for 5 minutes.

5 Add the pancetta and cook until golden. Add the puréed sweetcorn mixture, the milk, cream, potatoes and remaining sweetcorn. Bring to the boil, then lower the heat and simmer for 10–15 minutes, or until the potatoes are tender.

6 Season to taste with cayenne, salt and pepper, then stir in the tomatoes and lobster meat. Heat through without boiling and serve in warmed soup bowls.

Hot and Spicy Soups

The robust flavours of a wealth of cuisines are featured in these exotic recipes – sweet and aromatic Middle Eastern; fragrant and zesty Asian; piquant and fruity Caribbean; and out-and-out fiery Mexican.

Roasted tomato and chilli soup with black olive cream

serves **4–6**
preparation time **30 minutes**
cooking time **about 1¼ hours**

1.5 kg (3 lb) ripe tomatoes,
  preferably plum
6 tablespoons olive oil
1½ teaspoons sea salt
1 tablespoon caster sugar
1 large red chilli
3–4 shallots or 1 onion, chopped
1 garlic clove, crushed
600 ml (1 pint) water
2–4 tablespoons lime juice
salt and pepper

Olive cream
50 g (2 oz) pitted black olives
50 g (2 oz) crème fraîche

1 Cut the tomatoes in half lengthways and, holding each half over a bowl, scoop out the seeds with a teaspoon. Reserve the tomato seeds and any juice.

2 Lightly grease a baking sheet with a little of the oil and lay the tomatoes on it, cut-side up. Sprinkle them with about 4 tablespoons of the remaining oil, the sea salt and sugar. Add the chilli and put the baking sheet in a preheated oven, 180°C (350°F), Gas Mark 4, for 45–50 minutes. Remove the chilli after 20 minutes, when it is well charred and blistered. When cool, peel, deseed and chop it roughly.

3 Meanwhile, to make the olive cream, chop the olives very finely, fold them into the crème fraîche and season to taste with salt and pepper.

4 Heat the remaining oil in a saucepan over a moderate heat, add the shallots or onion and cook for 6–8 minutes, or until lightly golden and softened. Add the garlic and cook for a further 2 minutes.

5 Add the roasted tomatoes with any liquid from the baking sheet, the reserved seeds and juice, the chilli and the measured water. Bring the soup to the boil, then lower the heat and simmer for 10–12 minutes.

6 Purée the soup in a blender or food processor. Strain through a sieve and return to the pan to reheat. Season to taste with salt, pepper and lime juice. Serve the soup in warmed bowls with a spoonful of the olive cream in each bowl.

Split pea soup with chorizo

serves **6–8**
preparation time **15–20 minutes**, plus soaking
cooking time **about 2 hours**

375 g (12 oz) split yellow peas, soaked overnight in cold water to cover
2 tablespoons olive oil
3 chorizo sausages, thinly sliced
1 onion, chopped
2 garlic cloves, finely chopped
1.2 litres (2 pints) Chicken Stock (see page 9)
900 ml (1 1/2 pints) water
1 bay leaf
1 thyme sprig or 1/4 teaspoon dried thyme
3 carrots, quartered lengthways and thinly sliced
salt

1 Drain the soaked split peas in a colander, rinse under cold running water and drain again.

2 Heat the oil in a large saucepan. Cook the chorizo sausages over a moderate heat, stirring, for 5 minutes. With a slotted spoon, transfer the slices to kitchen paper to drain. Pour off all but 1 tablespoon of the fat in the pan.

3 Add the onion and garlic to the pan and cook over a moderate heat until softened. Add the drained split peas, stock, measured water, bay leaf and thyme. Bring the mixture to the boil, skimming off the scum as it rises to the surface with a slotted spoon. Lower the heat and simmer, partially covered, for 1 1/4 hours. Stir the mixture occasionally.

4 Add the carrots and cook for a further 30 minutes, or until tender. Season to taste with salt. Remove and discard the bay leaf, add the reserved chorizo and cook for a further 10 minutes. Serve in warmed soup bowls.

White bean soup
with toasted garlic and chilli oil

serves **6**
preparation time **35 minutes**,
plus soaking
cooking time **1–1¼ hours**

250 g (8 oz) dried white beans
(haricot, cannellini, etc.), soaked
overnight in cold water to cover
Vegetable or Chicken Stock (see
pages 8 and 9), or cold water,
to cover
handful of sage leaves
4 garlic cloves
150 ml (¼ pint) olive oil
2 tablespoons chopped sage or
rosemary
good pinch of chilli flakes
salt and pepper
roughly chopped parsley, to garnish

1 Drain the beans and put them into a flameproof casserole. Cover with the stock or water to a depth of 5 cm (2 inches) above the beans and push in the sage leaves. Bring the beans to the boil, then cover them tightly and bake in a preheated oven, 160°C (325°F), Gas Mark 3, for 40-60 minutes, depending on their freshness. Leave them in their cooking liquid.

2 Meanwhile, finely chop half the garlic and thinly slice the remainder.

3 Put half the beans, the cooked sage and all the liquid into a blender or food processor and blend until smooth. Pour the purée back into the casserole with the remaining beans. If the soup is thicker than liked, add extra water or stock to thin it.

4 Heat half the oil in a frying pan and add the chopped garlic. Cook gently until it is soft and golden, then add the chopped sage or rosemary and cook for 30 seconds. Stir the mixture into the soup and reheat until boiling. Simmer gently for 10 minutes. Taste and season well with salt and pepper. Pour into a warmed tureen or ladle into warmed soup bowls.

5 Cook the sliced garlic carefully in the remaining oil until golden (don't let it become too dark or it will be bitter), then stir in the chilli flakes. Dip the base of the pan into cold water to stop the garlic cooking, then spoon the garlic and oil over the soup. Serve sprinkled with chopped parsley.

Harira

serves **8–10**

preparation time **about 25 minutes**, plus soaking

cooking time **about 3 hours**

250 g (8 oz) chickpeas, soaked for 48 hours in cold water to cover or 12 hours if covered with boiling water

2 chicken breasts, halved

1.2 litres (2 pints) Chicken Stock (see page 9)

1.2 litres (2 pints) water

2 x 425 g (14 oz) cans chopped tomatoes

¼ teaspoon crumbled saffron threads

2 onions, chopped

125 g (4 oz) long-grain white rice

50 g (2 oz) green lentils, rinsed and drained

2 tablespoons finely chopped fresh coriander

2 tablespoons finely chopped parsley

salt and pepper

1 Drain the chickpeas in a colander, rinse and drain again. Put them into a saucepan, cover with water to a depth of 5 cm (2 inches) above the chickpeas and bring to the boil. Lower the heat and simmer, partially covered, for 2 hours, or until the chickpeas are tender, adding more water as necessary. Drain and set aside.

2 Put the chicken breasts, stock and measured water in a separate saucepan. Bring to the boil, then lower the heat, cover and simmer for 10–15 minutes, or until the chicken is just cooked. Remove the chicken and shred it, discarding the skin and any bones. Set aside.

3 Add the chickpeas, tomatoes, saffron, onions, rice and lentils to the stock in the pan. Simmer, covered, for 30–35 minutes, or until the rice and lentils are tender.

4 Add the shredded chicken, coriander and parsley, and heat for 5 minutes without boiling. Season with salt and pepper and serve in warmed soup bowls.

Chilli bean and pepper soup

serves **6**
preparation time **20 minutes**
cooking time **40 minutes**

2 tablespoons sunflower oil
1 large onion, finely chopped
4 garlic cloves, finely chopped
2 red peppers, cored, deseeded
  and diced
2 red chillies, deseeded and finely
  chopped
900 ml (1½ pints) Vegetable Stock
  (see page 8)
750 ml (1¼ pints) tomato juice or
  passata (sieved tomatoes)
1 tablespoon double-concentrate
  tomato purée
1 tablespoon sun-dried tomato
  paste
2 tablespoons sweet chilli sauce,
  or more to taste
400 g (13 oz) can red kidney
  beans, drained
2 tablespoons finely chopped fresh
  coriander
salt and pepper
lime rind strips, to garnish
  (optional)

To serve
75 ml (3 fl oz) soured cream or
  crème fraîche
tortilla chips

1 Heat the oil in a large saucepan, add the onion and garlic and cook until soft but not coloured. Stir in the red peppers and chillies and fry for a few minutes. Stir in the stock and tomato juice or passata, tomato purée and paste, chilli sauce, beans and coriander. Bring to the boil, then lower the heat, cover and simmer for 30 minutes.

2 Cool slightly, then purée in a blender or food processor until smooth. Return the soup to the pan and taste and adjust the seasoning if necessary. Bring to the boil and serve in warmed soup bowls. Stir a little soured cream or crème fraîche into each portion and garnish with lime rind strips, if liked. Serve with tortilla chips.

Green lentil soup with spiced butter

serves **4**
preparation time **10 minutes**
cooking time **25–30 minutes**

2 tablespoons olive oil
2 onions, chopped
2 bay leaves
175 g (6 oz) green lentils, rinsed
   and drained
1 litre (1³/₄ pints) Vegetable Stock
   (see page 8)
¹/₂ teaspoon ground turmeric
small handful of fresh coriander
   leaves, roughly chopped
salt and pepper

Spiced butter
50 g (2 oz) lightly salted butter,
   softened
1 large garlic clove, crushed
1 tablespoon chopped fresh
   coriander
1 teaspoon paprika
1 teaspoon cumin seeds
1 red chilli, deseeded and finely
   chopped

1 Heat the oil in a large saucepan, add the onions and cook for 3 minutes. Add the bay leaves, lentils, stock and turmeric. Bring to the boil, then lower the heat, cover and simmer for 20 minutes, or until the lentils are tender and turning mushy.

2 Meanwhile, to make the spiced butter, beat the butter with the garlic, coriander, paprika, cumin and chilli and transfer the mixture to a small serving dish.

3 Stir the coriander leaves into the soup, season to taste with salt and pepper and serve in warmed soup bowls with the spiced butter in a separate bowl for stirring into the soup.

Red pepper and spicy chicken soup

serves **4**

preparation time **20 minutes**, plus cooling

cooking time **50 minutes**

3 red peppers, halved, cored and deseeded

1 red onion, quartered

2 garlic cloves, unpeeled

2 teaspoons five-spice powder

150 g (5 oz) boneless, skinless chicken breast

1 teaspoon olive oil

5 cm (2 inch) piece of fresh root ginger, grated

1 teaspoon ground cumin

1 teaspoon ground coriander

1 large potato, chopped

900 ml (1½ pints) Chicken Stock (see page 9)

salt and pepper

4 tablespoons fromage frais, to serve

1 Place the peppers, onion and garlic cloves in a nonstick roasting tin. Roast in a preheated oven, 200°C (400°F), Gas Mark 6, for 40 minutes, or until the peppers have blistered and the onion quarters and garlic are very soft. If the onion quarters start to brown too much, cover them with the pepper halves.

2 Meanwhile, scatter the five-spice powder over the chicken breast and grill under a medium heat for 20 minutes until crisp. When cooked, cut the chicken into thin shreds and put aside.

3 While the chicken is grilling, heat the oil in a saucepan and fry the ginger, cumin and coriander over a low heat for 5 minutes, until softened. Add the potato and stir well, season and pour in the chicken stock. Simmer, covered, for 30 minutes.

4 Remove the cooked vegetables from the oven. Place the peppers in a polythene bag. Tie the top and leave to cool. (The steam produced in the bag makes it easier to remove the skin when cool.) Add the onions to the potato mixture and carefully squeeze out the garlic pulp into the saucepan, too. Peel the peppers and add to the soup. Simmer for 5 minutes.

5 Pour the soup into a blender or food processor and blend, in batches if necessary, for a few seconds until quite smooth. Return to the saucepan and thin with a little water, if necessary, to achieve the desired consistency. Stir the shredded chicken into the soup and simmer for 5 minutes.

6 Spoon into warmed bowls and top each one with a spoonful of fromage frais.

Spiced chickpea and lamb soup

serves **6**
preparation time **10 minutes**,
plus soaking
cooking time **2½ hours**

50 g (2 oz) chickpeas, soaked
    overnight in cold water to cover
50 g (2 oz) black-eyed beans,
    soaked overnight in cold water
    to cover
50 g (2 oz) trahana or bulgar
    wheat
500 g (1 lb) neck of lamb, cut into
    4 pieces
4 tablespoons olive oil
1 onion, chopped
2 carrots, chopped
425 g (14 oz) can chopped
    tomatoes
4 small red chillies
4 thyme sprigs
1 teaspoon each ground coriander,
    cumin and cinnamon
½ teaspoon each dried mint and
    oregano
salt and pepper

To serve
olive oil
crusty bread

1 Drain the soaked peas and beans in a colander, rinse under cold running water and drain again. Put them into separate saucepans, cover with plenty of cold water and bring to the boil. Lower the heat and simmer for 1 hour, then drain and reserve the liquid.

2 Place the cooked pulses in a clay pot or casserole dish, add all the remaining ingredients and cover with the reserved liquid, adding extra water to cover, if necessary.

3 Cover the casserole with a tight-fitting lid and bake in a preheated oven, 180°C (350°F), Gas Mark 4, for 1½ hours, or until the meat and vegetables are tender.

4 Serve each bowl of soup drizzled with olive oil and pass around some crusty bread.

Mexican soup with avocado salsa

serves **4**
preparation time **about**
20 minutes
cooking time **45 minutes**

2 tablespoons sunflower oil
1 large onion, chopped
2 garlic cloves, crushed
2 teaspoons ground coriander
1 teaspoon ground cumin
1 red pepper, cored, deseeded
  and diced
3 red chillies, deseeded and sliced
425 g (14 oz) can red kidney
  beans, drained and rinsed
750 ml (1¼ pints) tomato juice
1–2 tablespoons chilli sauce
25 g (1 oz) tortilla chips, crushed
salt and pepper
fresh coriander sprigs, to garnish

Avocado salsa
1 small ripe avocado
4 spring onions, finely chopped
1 tablespoon lemon juice
1 tablespoon chopped fresh
  coriander
salt and pepper

1 Heat the oil in a large saucepan. Add the onion, garlic, spices, red pepper and two-thirds of the chillies and cook gently for 10 minutes. Add the beans, tomato juice and chilli sauce. Bring to the boil, then lower the heat, cover and simmer gently for 30 minutes.

2 Meanwhile, to make the avocado salsa, peel, stone and finely dice the avocado. Put into a bowl and combine it with the spring onions, lemon juice and fresh coriander. Season to taste with salt and pepper, cover the bowl with clingfilm and set aside.

3 Purée the soup in a blender or food processor, together with the crushed tortilla chips. Return the soup to a clean saucepan, season with salt and pepper to taste and heat through. Serve immediately in warmed soup bowls with the avocado salsa. Garnish with the reserved chilli slices and the coriander sprigs.

Jamaican pepperpot soup

serves **6–8**
preparation time **30–35 minutes**
cooking time **about 1¼ hours**

1 kg (2 lb) lean stewing beef, cut
   into small cubes
250 g (8 oz) lean pork, cut into
   small cubes
2.5 litres (4 pints) water
24 okra, conical stalk end
   discarded and roughly chopped.
500 g (1 lb) kale, roughly chopped
500 g (1 lb) spinach, stems
   discarded and leaves roughly
   chopped
2 green peppers, cored, deseeded
   and roughly chopped
2 spring onions, roughly chopped
1 fresh thyme sprig or ¼ teaspoon
   dried thyme
¼ teaspoon cayenne pepper
500 g (1 lb) yellow yams, thinly
   sliced
1 large potato, thinly sliced
1 garlic clove, crushed or finely
   chopped
salt

1 Combine the meat with the measured water in a large saucepan. Bring to the boil, then lower the heat and simmer the meat, partially covered, for about 30 minutes.

2 Add the okra, kale, spinach, green peppers and spring onions to the pan with the thyme and cayenne. Cook over a moderate heat, partially covered, for 15 minutes.

3 Add the yams, potato and garlic to the pan and cook for a further 20 minutes, or until the yams and potato are soft. Add more water if the soup is too thick. Season to taste with salt. Serve the soup hot in a warmed soup tureen.

Callaloo

serves **6**
preparation time **15 minutes**
cooking time **35 minutes**

3 tablespoons groundnut oil
1 large onion, finely chopped
4 spring onions, finely chopped
2 garlic cloves, crushed
1 red chilli, deseeded and finely
  chopped
1 teaspoon turmeric
1 thyme sprig, crumbled
250 g (8 oz) okra, thinly sliced
500 g (1 lb) fresh callaloo or
  spinach leaves, hard stems
  discarded and roughly chopped
900 ml (1½ pints) Vegetable or
  Chicken Stock (see pages 8
  and 9)
a few saffron threads
425 ml (14 fl oz) coconut milk
250 g (8 oz) crab meat, fresh or
  canned
juice of ½ lime
dash of hot pepper sauce
salt and pepper

1 Heat the oil in a large saucepan, add the onion, spring onions and garlic and cook gently for 5 minutes, or until softened. Add the chilli, turmeric and thyme and stir over a low heat for 1–2 minutes.

2 Stir in the okra, then add the callaloo or spinach leaves. Turn up the heat and cook, stirring, until the leaves start to wilt. Lower the heat and add the stock and saffron. Bring to the boil, then lower the heat, cover and simmer for 20 minutes.

3 Add the coconut milk and crab meat and stir well. Heat gently for 4–5 minutes and then season to taste with salt and pepper. Just before serving, stir in the lime juice and hot pepper sauce.

Moroccan fish soup

serves **6–8**
preparation time **about 35 minutes**
cooking time **about 40 minutes**

3 tablespoons olive oil
2 onions, chopped
2 celery sticks, sliced
4 garlic cloves, crushed
1 red chilli, deseeded and chopped
$\frac{1}{2}$ teaspoon ground cumin
1 cinnamon stick
$\frac{1}{2}$ teaspoon ground coriander
2 large potatoes, chopped
1.5 litres (2$\frac{1}{2}$ pints) Fish Stock (see page 10) or water
3 tablespoons lemon juice
2 kg (4 lb) mixed fish and shellfish, prepared
4 well-flavoured tomatoes, skinned, deseeded if liked and chopped
1 large bunch of mixed dill, parsley and fresh coriander, chopped
salt and pepper

1 Heat the oil in a large saucepan. Add the onion and celery and cook gently until softened and transparent, adding the garlic and chilli towards the end. Add the cumin, cinnamon and ground coriander and stir for 1 minute, then add the potatoes and cook, stirring, for a further 2 minutes.

2 Add the stock or water and the lemon juice and simmer gently, uncovered, for about 20 minutes, or until the potatoes are tender.

3 Add the fish and shellfish, the tomatoes, herbs and salt and pepper to taste and cook gently until the fish and shellfish are tender. Serve in warmed soup bowls.

tip Any selection of fish and shellfish can be used for fish soup, with the exception of oily fish such as mackerel and sardines. The trimmings, heads, tails, bones and shells can be used to make the fish stock.

Wonton soup

serves **4**
preparation time **25 minutes**
cooking time **15 minutes**

20 wonton wrappers
1.2 litres (2 pints) Chicken Stock
   (see page 9)
2 pink Asian shallots or 1 small
   onion, finely chopped
2.5 cm (1 inch) piece of fresh root
   ginger, peeled and finely sliced
1 teaspoon caster sugar
4 spring onions, finely sliced
½ tablespoon light soy sauce
1 teaspoon rice vinegar
handful of roughly chopped parsley
1 teaspoon sesame oil
salt and pepper
chilli oil, to serve

Filling
125 g (4 oz) white fish or prawns
125 g (4 oz) white crab meat
2 spring onions, finely chopped
2.5 cm (1 inch) piece of fresh
   root ginger, peeled and
   finely chopped
1 garlic clove, crushed

1 First make the filling. Chop the fish or prawns and crab meat very finely with the spring onions, chopped ginger and garlic or put all the ingredients in a blender or food processor and blend to a paste.

2 Put 1 teaspoon of the mixture on a wonton wrapper, brush around the filling with a little water and fold the wrapper over to make a triangle. Repeat with the remaining mixture until all the wontons are made. Keep the wrappers covered with a damp cloth to prevent them from drying out before you fill them.

3 Put the stock into a saucepan with the shallots or small onion and sliced ginger and bring to the boil. Lower the heat and add the sugar and filled wontons. Simmer gently for 5 minutes.

4 Add the spring onions, soy sauce, vinegar, parsley and salt and pepper to taste. Just before serving, add the sesame oil. Serve the soup in warmed bowls accompanied by small dishes of chilli oil.

Hot and sour prawn noodle soup

serves **4**
preparation time **20 minutes**, plus soaking
cooking time **35–40 minutes**

500 g (1 lb) raw large prawns in their shells, defrosted if frozen
1 tablespoon sunflower oil
2 spring onions, roughly chopped
2.5 cm (1 inch) piece of fresh root ginger, peeled and chopped
1 small red or green chilli, deseeded and finely chopped
2 Kaffir lime leaves or rind from 1 lime, cut into strips
2 lemon grass stalks, bruised and chopped into 2.5 cm (1 inch) pieces, or 1 tablespoon dried chopped lemon grass, soaked in hot water to cover for 30 minutes
1.2 litres (2 pints) Chicken Stock (see page 9)
2–4 tablespoons lime juice
75 g (3 oz) fine egg or rice noodles
125 g (4 oz) small oyster mushrooms

To garnish
2 spring onions, cut into thin strips
fresh coriander sprigs

1 Peel and devein the prawns, reserving the shells. Rinse the prawns and set aside.

2 Heat the oil in a large saucepan, add the chopped spring onions, ginger and chilli and cook gently, without colouring, for 5 minutes. Add the reserved prawn shells and cook for 3 minutes, then add the lime leaves or rind, lemon grass (if using dried lemon grass, add it with its soaking liquid), stock and 2 tablespoons lime juice. Bring to the boil, then lower the heat and simmer gently for 20 minutes.

3 Meanwhile, cook the noodles according to the packet instructions, drain and set aside.

4 Strain the stock through a fine sieve into a clean pan. Taste and add more lime juice if required. Bring back to the boil, then lower the heat, add the prawns and cook for about 2 minutes, or until opaque. Add the mushrooms and cook for 1–2 minutes, or until just soft. Add the noodles and heat through. Serve in warmed soup bowls, sprinkled with spring onion strips and coriander sprigs.

Malaysian laksa

serves **4**
preparation time **15 minutes**
cooking time **25–30 minutes**

3 tablespoons groundnut oil
2 large onions, finely chopped
4 garlic cloves, crushed
3 red bird's eye chillies, finely
   chopped
75 g (3 oz) roasted peanuts,
   chopped
1 tablespoon ground coriander
1 tablespoon ground cumin
2 teaspoons turmeric
1.2 litres (2 pints) coconut milk
1 teaspoon shrimp paste
1–2 tablespoons sugar, to taste
375 g (12 oz) cooked chicken,
   shredded
175 g (6 oz) bean sprouts
500 g (1 lb) fresh flat rice noodles
4 spring onions, chopped
3 tablespoons chopped fresh
   coriander leaves
salt and pepper

To serve
4 spring onions, chopped
1 large red chilli, finely sliced
1–2 tablespoons chopped roasted
   peanuts

1 Heat the oil in a saucepan, add the onions and cook until golden brown. Add the garlic, chillies, peanuts, ground coriander, cumin and turmeric and cook for 2–3 minutes, or until the spices have cooked through and released a strong aroma.

2 Stir the coconut milk and shrimp paste into the spice mixture, cover and simmer for 15 minutes. Season the spiced coconut with salt, pepper and sugar to taste. Add the shredded chicken and half the bean sprouts and simmer for 5 minutes.

3 Blanch the noodles in boiling water and divide between 4 large bowls. Sprinkle with the spring onions and fresh coriander and divide the remaining raw bean sprouts between the bowls.

4 Ladle the chicken and coconut mixture over the noodles and serve with spring onions, red chilli and roasted peanuts, in separate bowls for garnishing.

Beef and flat noodle soup

serves **4–6**
preparation time **25 minutes**
cooking time **2¼ hours**

500 g (1 lb) chuck steak
1.8 litres (3 pints) Beef Stock
    (see page 11) or water
4 star anise
1 large cinnamon stick
1 teaspoon black peppercorns
2 sweet onions or 4 shallots,
    thinly sliced
4 garlic cloves, crushed
7 cm (3 inch) piece of fresh root
    ginger, finely sliced
125 g (4 oz) bean sprouts
250 g (8 oz) dried flat rice noodles
6 spring onions, thinly sliced
handful of fresh coriander leaves
250 g (8 oz) fillet of beef, thinly
    sliced
2 tablespoons fish sauce
salt and pepper
red bird's eye chillies, to garnish

Nuoc cham sauce
2 red chillies, chopped
1 garlic clove
1½ tablespoons caster sugar
1 tablespoon lime juice
1 tablespoon rice vinegar
3 tablespoons fish sauce
4 tablespoons water

To serve
bean sprouts
thin spring onions, sliced
1 large red chilli, sliced

1 Heat a large dry frying pan until very hot and sear the chuck steak on all sides until brown and charred.

2 Put the beef into a large saucepan with the stock or water, star anise, cinnamon, black peppercorns, 1 sliced onion or 2 shallots, the garlic and ginger. Bring to the boil, skimming off any scum that rises to the surface with a slotted spoon, and continue to boil for about 10 minutes. Lower the heat, cover and simmer for about 2 hours, or until the beef is tender.

3 Blanch the bean sprouts in boiling water for 1 minute.

4 Cook the noodles in boiling water for 3–4 minutes, or until just soft. Do not overcook them. Drain well and put into 4 large soup bowls. Arrange the bean sprouts, spring onions, coriander leaves and the remaining onions or shallots over the noodles.

5 To make the nuoc cham sauce, pound the chopped chillies, garlic and sugar until smooth, using a pestle and mortar. Add the lime juice, vinegar, fish sauce and measured water and blend together well. Put the mixture into a small bowl.

6 When the beef from the broth is tender, lift it out, slice it thinly and divide it between the soup bowls with the slices of raw fillet and garnish with the red bird's eye chillies.

7 Strain the broth, return it to the pan and season to taste with fish sauce, salt and pepper. To serve, ladle the hot broth over the contents of the bowls and serve immediately with the nuoc cham sauce and a plate of extra bean sprouts, spring onions and red chilli.

Winter Warmers

The perfect meal-in-a-bowl, there is nothing more comforting and satisfying than soup. These hearty dishes are thick with root vegetables, pulses and grains, and include delicious toppings, such as garlic croûtons, grated cheese or soured cream.

Cream of celeriac soup with porcini dumplings

serves **4–6**
preparation time **25 minutes**,
plus soaking and chilling
cooking time **35–40 minutes**

50 g (2 oz) butter
2 shallots or 1 onion, chopped
1 garlic clove, crushed
500 g (1 lb) celeriac, cut into
  small dice
900 ml (1½ pints) Vegetable or
  Chicken Stock (see pages 8
  and 9)
300 ml (½ pint) single cream
  or milk
salt and pepper
finely grated Parmesan cheese,
  to serve

Dumplings
5 g (¼ oz) dried porcini
  mushrooms (ceps)
25 g (1 oz) butter
1 shallot, finely chopped
175 g (6 oz) ricotta cheese
25 g (1 oz) finely grated Parmesan
  cheese
2 egg yolks, beaten
2 tablespoons plain flour, plus
  extra for rolling
1 tablespoon chopped parsley

1 To make the dumplings, put the porcini into a small bowl and pour over warm water to cover. Leave to soak for 30 minutes. Drain in a fine sieve, reserving the liquid. Rinse the mushrooms well in cold water, chop finely and set aside.

2 Melt the butter in a small saucepan over a low heat, add the shallot and cook gently, without colouring, for 5–6 minutes, or until softened. Spoon into a bowl, add the remaining ingredients and mix to form a soft dough. Season to taste with salt and pepper. Cover and refrigerate for 30–60 minutes. With lightly floured hands, form the mixture into about 30 small balls, roll in flour and put on to a tray.

3 Meanwhile, to make the soup, melt the butter in a saucepan over a moderate heat, add the shallots or onion and garlic and cook, without colouring, for 5 minutes. Add the celeriac, cover and cook for 5–10 minutes, or until the celeriac begins to soften. Add the stock and bring to the boil, then lower the heat and simmer for 10–15 minutes.

4 Purée the soup in a blender or food processor until smooth. Return the soup to the pan, stir in the cream or milk and season to taste. Reheat without boiling.

5 Bring a saucepan of lightly salted water to the boil. Add the dumplings and simmer for 3–4 minutes. Drain well and add to the soup just before serving. Serve in warmed soup bowls, sprinkled with grated Parmesan.

Chestnut soup

serves **6**

preparation time **20 minutes**,
plus soaking (if using dried
chestnuts)

cooking time **45 minutes–1 hour**

750 g (1¹/₂ lb) fresh, plump, sweet
　　chestnuts or 400 g (13 oz) dried
　　chestnuts, soaked overnight in
　　cold water to cover
125 g (4 oz) butter
150 g (5 oz) pancetta or streaky
　　bacon, chopped
2 onions, finely chopped
1 carrot, chopped
1 celery stick, chopped
2 garlic cloves, halved
1 tablespoon chopped rosemary
2 bay leaves
salt and pepper
rosemary sprigs, to garnish

1 If you are using fresh chestnuts, use a small sharp knife to slit the shell of each chestnut across the rounded side. Put them into a saucepan and cover with cold water. Bring to the boil, then lower the heat and simmer for 15–20 minutes. Lift out the chestnuts and discard the water. Peel off the thick outer skin and the thinner inner skin, which has a bitter taste.

2 Melt the butter in a large saucepan and add the pancetta or bacon. Cook over a moderate heat until beginning to turn golden. Add the onions, carrot and celery and cook for 5–10 minutes, or until softened.

3 Add the chestnuts to the pan (including the soaking water from dried chestnuts) with the garlic, rosemary and bay leaves and enough water to cover completely. Bring to the boil then simmer for 30 minutes, stirring occasionally. Season with salt and pepper. Serve in warmed bowls, garnished with rosemary.

Sweet potato soup

serves **6–8**
preparation time **15 minutes**
cooking time **50 minutes–1 hour**

4–6 rindless smoked bacon rashers
25 g (1 oz) butter
1 onion, chopped
2 carrots, sliced
2 celery sticks, sliced
1 bay leaf
750 g (1½ lb) sweet potatoes,
  sliced
250 g (8 oz) potatoes, sliced
1.2 litres (2 pints) Chicken Stock
  (see page 9)
150 ml (¼ pint) water
125 ml (4 fl oz) dry white wine
¼ teaspoon grated nutmeg
¼ teaspoon white pepper
salt

1 Heat the bacon in a frying pan over a gentle heat until the fat runs, then raise the heat and cook over a moderate heat until very crisp. Using tongs, transfer the bacon on to kitchen paper to drain.

2 Add the butter to the bacon fat left in the frying pan and cook the onion, carrots, celery and bay leaf over a low heat for 5–8 minutes, stirring frequently.

3 Transfer the mixture to a saucepan. Add the sweet potatoes, potatoes, stock, measured water and wine. Bring the mixture to the boil, then lower the heat and simmer, covered, for 35–40 minutes, or until the vegetables are very tender. Remove and discard the bay leaf.

4 Purée the mixture in a blender or food processor until smooth. Transfer to a clean saucepan. Add the nutmeg, white pepper and salt to taste. Put the pan over a moderate heat, stirring, until the soup is hot.

5 Serve the soup in warmed bowls, garnishing each portion with the reserved bacon.

Tomato and bread soup

serves **4**
preparation time **10 minutes**
cooking time **about 35 minutes**

1 kg (2 lb) vine-ripened tomatoes,
   skinned, deseeded and chopped
300 ml (½ pint) Vegetable Stock
   (see page 8)
6 tablespoons olive oil
2 garlic cloves, crushed
1 teaspoon sugar
2 tablespoons chopped basil
100 g (3⅓ oz) day-old bread,
   without crusts
1 tablespoon balsamic vinegar
salt and pepper
pesto, to serve (optional)

1 Put the tomatoes into a saucepan with the stock, 2 tablespoons of the oil, the garlic, sugar and basil and bring gradually to the boil. Lower the heat, cover and simmer gently for 30 minutes.

2 Crumble the bread into the soup and stir over a low heat until it has thickened. Stir in the balsamic vinegar and the remaining oil and season to taste with salt and pepper. Stir a spoonful of pesto into each bowl before serving, if liked.

Kale soup with garlic croûtons

serves **8–10**
preparation time **20–25 minutes**
cooking time **about 45 minutes**

50 g (2 oz) butter
1 onion, chopped
2 carrots, sliced
500 g (1 lb kale), thick stems
  discarded
1.2 litres (2 pints) water
600 ml (1 pint) Vegetable Stock
  (see page 8)
1 tablespoon lemon juice
300 g (10 oz) potatoes, sliced
pinch of grated nutmeg
salt and pepper
2 kale leaves, finely shredded,
  to garnish
garlic croûtons, to serve
  (see below)

1 Melt the butter in a large saucepan, add the onion and cook over a moderate heat until soft but not brown, stirring frequently. Add the carrots and kale in batches, stirring constantly. Cook for 2 minutes. Add the measured water, stock, lemon juice, potatoes, nutmeg and salt and pepper to taste. Bring to the boil, stirring from time to time. Lower the heat, cover and simmer for 30–35 minutes, or until all the vegetables are soft.

2 Purée the mixture in a blender or food processor until smooth. Transfer to a clean pan. If it is too thick, add some water.

3 Add the shredded kale leaves to the pan and cook, stirring constantly, until crisp.

4 Check the seasoning and reheat the soup without boiling. Serve in warmed soup bowls with the garlic croûtons and garnish with the crisp kale.

tip To make garlic croûtons, cut the crusts off 2 slices of white bread and gently rub the bread all over with the cut sides of a halved garlic clove, then cube the bread. Heat 1 tablespoon vegetable oil in a heavy-based frying pan and fry the bread cubes, turning and stirring frequently, for 1–2 minutes, or until golden and crisp.

Pumpkin and apple soup

serves **4–5**
preparation time **15 minutes**
cooking time **30 minutes**

2 tablespoons butter
1 large onion, roughly chopped
2 teaspoons chopped fresh thyme
2 small cooking apples, peeled,
   cored and roughly chopped
3 tablespoons dark soft brown
   sugar
2 tablespoons whole-grain
   mustard
1 small pumpkin, about 750 g
   (1½ lb), skinned, deseeded and
   cut into chunks
1 litre (1¾ pints) Vegetable Stock
   (see page 8)
125 g (4 oz) crème fraîche
salt and pepper
pumpkin seeds, to serve

1 Melt the butter in a large saucepan. Add the onion and thyme and cook gently, stirring frequently, for about 5 minutes, or until softened and beginning to colour. Add the apples and sugar and cook gently for a further 3 minutes.

2 Add the mustard, pumpkin and stock and bring just to the boil. Lower the heat, cover and simmer gently for about 20 minutes, or until the pumpkin and apples are very soft and falling apart.

3 Purée the mixture in a blender or food processor until smooth.

4 Stir in half the crème fraîche, season to taste with salt and pepper and heat through gently. Ladle into warmed soup bowls, spoon over the remaining crème fraîche and serve sprinkled with pumpkin seeds.

Oven-baked vegetable soup

serves **4**
preparation time **15 minutes**
cooking time **about 1¼ hours**

1 onion, roughly chopped
2 garlic cloves, chopped
2 large carrots, thinly sliced
1 leek, thickly sliced
1 large parsnip, diced
175 g (6 oz) swede, diced
4 tablespoons olive oil
2 teaspoons clear honey
4 thyme sprigs
4 rosemary sprigs
2 bay leaves
4 ripe tomatoes, quartered
1.2 litres (2 pints) Vegetable Stock
   (see page 8)
salt and pepper
buttered toast, to serve

1 Toss the vegetables with the oil and honey and put into a roasting tin. Add the herbs and transfer to a preheated oven, 200°C (400°F), Gas Mark 6. Roast for about 50–60 minutes, or until all the vegetables are golden and tender. Add the tomatoes halfway through cooking. Lower the oven temperature to 190°C (375°F), Gas Mark 5.

2 Remove and discard the herbs and transfer the vegetables to a blender or food processor. Add half the stock and process until smooth, then blend in the remaining stock.

3 Transfer the soup to a casserole dish, season to taste with salt and pepper and bake for 20 minutes, or until heated through. Serve in warmed soup bowls with buttered toast.

Country bean and vegetable broth

serves **4**
preparation time **10 minutes**,
plus soaking
cooking time **about 1¼ hours**

25 g (1 oz) each dried kidney
beans, pinto beans and black-
eyed beans, soaked overnight in
cold water to cover, drained
and rinsed
25 g (1 oz) dried porcini
mushrooms (ceps)
1 tablespoon olive oil
2 shallots, finely chopped
2 garlic cloves, crushed
125 g (4 oz) button mushrooms,
diced
2 tablespoons chopped mixed fresh
herbs, plus extra to garnish
50 g (2 oz) mini pasta shapes
1.2 litres (2 pints) hot Beef Stock
(see page 11)
salt and pepper

1 Put the beans into a large saucepan with water to
cover. Bring to the boil and boil vigorously for
10 minutes. Skim any scum that rises to the surface of
the liquid with a slotted spoon and lower the heat.
Simmer, covered, for 1 hour, or until all the beans are
very tender.

2 Meanwhile, put the dried mushrooms into a
heatproof bowl, cover with boiling water and set aside
for 15 minutes, then drain and reserve the liquid.

3 Heat the oil in a large saucepan, add the shallots
and garlic and cook for 3 minutes. Add the fresh
mushrooms and stir well. Add the herbs and pasta
shapes. Drain the beans and add them to the saucepan
with the hot stock, reserved mushroom liquid and salt
and pepper to taste. Bring to the boil, then lower the
heat and simmer for about 12 minutes. Serve
immediately in warmed bowls, sprinkled with chopped
herbs to garnish.

Tasty bean soup

serves **4**
preparation time **30 minutes**, plus soaking
cooking time **about 2¼ hours**

375 g (12 oz) dried haricot beans, soaked overnight in cold water to cover
2 litres (3½ pints water)
1 carrot, chopped
1 onion, quartered
1 bouquet garni
125 g (4 oz) cooked smoked ham, diced
40 g (1½ oz) butter
2 shallots, finely chopped
1 garlic clove, crushed
1 tablespoon chopped parsley
salt and pepper
parsley sprigs, to garnish
125 g (4 oz) croûtons, to serve (see page 18)

1 Drain the beans in a colander, rinse under cold running water and drain again.

2 Put the beans into a large saucepan with the measured water and bring to the boil over a moderate heat. Boil for 1½ hours, or until the beans are just tender. Add the carrot, onion, bouquet garni and ham and simmer for 20–30 minutes. Remove and discard the bouquet garni. Purée the soup in a blender or food processor until smooth. Return to the pan and reheat over a moderate heat.

3 Melt the butter in a heavy-based saucepan, add the shallots and garlic and cook gently until golden but not brown. Add the parsley and mix together quickly. Add the shallot mixture to the bean purée.

4 Mix well with a wooden spoon, season well with salt and pepper, then pour into warmed soup bowls. Sprinkle with croûtons and garnish with parsley sprigs.

Goulash soup

serves **6–8**
preparation time **10–15 minutes**
cooking time **1¼ hours**

3 tablespoons vegetable oil
750 g (1½ lb) boneless lean beef,
  cut into 2.5 cm (1 inch) strips
2 onions, chopped
2 garlic cloves, crushed
2 celery sticks, sliced
3 tablespoons paprika
1 tablespoon caraway seeds
1.2 litres (2 pints) Beef Stock
  (see page 11)
600 ml (1 pint) water
¼ teaspoon dried thyme
2 bay leaves
¼ teaspoon Tabasco sauce,
  or to taste
3 tablespoons tomato purée
250 g (8 oz) potatoes, cut into
  1 cm (½ inch) dice
3 carrots, cut into 1 cm (½ inch)
  dice
6–8 teaspoons soured cream,
  to garnish (optional)

1 Heat the oil in a large saucepan and brown the meat in batches over a moderate heat. As each batch browns, transfer it to kitchen paper to drain. Add the onions, garlic and celery to the remaining oil and cook until transparent.

2 Take the pan off the heat and stir in the paprika, caraway seeds, stock and the measured water. Add the thyme, bay leaves, Tabasco and tomato purée. Stir well and add the cooked beef. Bring the mixture to the boil, then lower the heat and simmer, partially covered, for 30 minutes.

3 Add the diced potatoes and carrots, then simmer for a further 30 minutes, or until the potatoes are tender. Remove and discard the bay leaves. Serve the soup immediately in warmed bowls, garnishing each portion with a teaspoon of soured cream, if liked.

Spanish chickpea soup

serves **8–10**
preparation time **15 minutes**,
plus soaking
cooking time **2½–2¾ hours**

150 g (5 oz) dried chickpeas,
  soaked for 48 hours in cold
  water to cover or 12 hours if
  covered with boiling water
1 small smoked, boneless bacon
  hock joint, about 500–750 g
  (1–1½ lb)
1 onion, studded with 4 cloves
2 garlic cloves, crushed
1 bay leaf
1 thyme sprig or ¼ teaspoon
  dried thyme
1 marjoram sprig or ½ teaspoon
  dried marjoram
1 parsley sprig
1.8 litres (3 pints) water
1.8 litres (3 pints) Chicken Stock
  (see page 9)
300–375 g (10–12 oz) potatoes,
  cut into 1 cm (½ inch) dice
300 g (10 oz) Savoy cabbage,
  shredded
salt and pepper

1 Drain the chickpeas in a colander, rinse under cold running water and drain again. Put the bacon joint into a deep saucepan and cover with cold water. Bring the water briefly to the boil, then drain, discarding the water.

2 Return the bacon joint to the clean saucepan. Add the chickpeas, onion, garlic, bay leaf, thyme, marjoram, parsley and the measured water. Bring the mixture to the boil, then lower the heat and simmer, partially covered, for 1½ hours. Remove and discard the onion, bay leaf and thyme, marjoram and parsley sprigs. Lift out the hock, put it on a board and cut it into small pieces. Set the pieces aside.

3 Add the stock, potatoes and cabbage to the pan and simmer for a further 30 minutes. Add the reserved hock pieces to the soup and cook for a further 10 minutes. Season to taste with salt and pepper. Serve in warmed soup bowls.

La Ribollita

serves **8**
preparation time **30 minutes**,
plus soaking and chilling
cooking time **about 3 hours**

150 ml (¼ pint) olive oil
1 onion, finely chopped
1 carrot, chopped
1 celery stick, chopped
2 leeks, finely chopped
4 garlic cloves, finely chopped
1 small white cabbage, shredded
1 large potato, chopped
4 courgettes, chopped
200 g (7 oz) dried cannellini beans,
   soaked overnight in cold water
   to cover, drained and rinsed
400 g (13 oz) passata (sieved
   tomatoes)
2 rosemary sprigs
2 thyme sprigs
2 sage sprigs
1 dried red chilli
2 litres (3½ pints) water
500 g (1 lb) cavolo nero (Tuscan
   black cabbage) or Savoy
   cabbage, finely shredded
6 thick slices of coarse crusty
   white bread
1 garlic clove, bruised
salt and pepper

To serve
olive oil
freshly grated Parmesan cheese

1 Heat half the oil in a large saucepan and add the onion, carrot and celery. Cook gently for about 10 minutes, stirring frequently. Add the leeks and finely chopped garlic and cook for a further 10 minutes. Add the white cabbage, potato and courgettes, stir well and cook for a further 10 minutes, stirring frequently.

2 Stir in the soaked beans, passata, rosemary, thyme and sage, dried chilli, salt to taste and plenty of black pepper. Cover with the measured water (the vegetables should be well covered) and bring to the boil, then lower the heat and simmer, covered, for at least 2 hours, or until the beans are very soft.

3 Remove 2–3 ladlefuls of soup, mash it well, then return to the pan. Stir in the cavolo nero or Savoy cabbage and simmer for a further 15 minutes. Leave the soup to cool, then cover and refrigerate overnight.

4 The next day, slowly reheat the soup, season if necessary and stir in the remaining oil. Toast the bread and rub it with the bruised garlic. Arrange the bread over the base of a tureen or in individual bowls and ladle the soup over it. Drizzle with oil and serve with plenty of freshly grated Parmesan.

Risi e bisi with frazzled prosciutto

serves **4**
preparation time **10 minutes**
cooking time **20–30 minutes**,
plus **5–10 minutes** for fresh peas

750 g (1½ lb) fresh young peas in the pod, shelled, or 250 g (8 oz) frozen peas, defrosted
3 tablespoons olive oil
1 onion, chopped
1.2 litres (2 pints) Chicken Stock (see page 9)
200 g (7 oz) risotto rice
large pinch of sugar
4 slices of prosciutto
2 tablespoons chopped flat leaf parsley
50 g (2 oz) Parmesan cheese, finely grated, plus extra to serve
salt and pepper

1 Heat 2 tablespoons of the oil in a large saucepan, add the onion and cook, without colouring, for 5–10 minutes, or until softened.

2 Add the stock and bring to the boil, then lower the heat and stir in the rice. (If using fresh peas, add them now and simmer gently for 5 minutes before adding the rice.) Season with salt and pepper and add the sugar. Cover and simmer gently, stirring occasionally, for 15–20 minutes, or until the rice is just tender. (If using frozen peas, add them after 10–15 minutes.)

3 Cut each slice of prosciutto in half lengthways. Heat the remaining oil in a large frying pan, add the prosciutto strips and cook over a high heat for 10–15 seconds, or until crisp. Drain on kitchen paper.

4 Stir the parsley and grated Parmesan into the soup. Serve in warmed soup bowls, topped with 2 pieces of the frazzled prosciutto and some grated Parmesan.

Barley soup with pork and cabbage

serves **6**
preparation time **15 minutes**
cooking time **55 minutes**

4 tablespoons olive oil
1 garlic clove, chopped
1 onion, chopped
1.2 litres (2 pints) Beef Stock
   (see page 11)
750 ml (1¼ pints) water
300 g (10 oz) lean pork, cut into
   1.5 cm (¾ inch) strips
2 carrots, chopped
300 g (10 oz) spring or Savoy
   cabbage, roughly chopped
125 g (4 oz) pearl barley
300 g (10 oz) potatoes, cut into
   1 cm (½ inch) dice
salt and pepper

1 Heat the oil in a large saucepan, add the garlic and onion and cook over a moderate heat until softened.

2 Add the stock, the measured water, pork, carrots, cabbage and barley. Bring the mixture to the boil, then lower the heat, cover and simmer for 20 minutes.

3 Add the potatoes with salt and pepper to taste. If the soup is too thick, add a little water. Replace the lid and simmer for a further 30 minutes. Stir from time to time. Serve in warmed soup bowls.

Gruyère soup with bacon and potatoes

serves **6–8**
preparation time **20 minutes**
cooking time **about 25 minutes**

2 tablespoons olive oil
3 rindless smoked bacon rashers,
  chopped
2 onions, finely chopped
600 ml (1 pint) Chicken Stock
  (see page 9)
900 ml (1½ pints) water
625 g (1¼ lb) potatoes, cut into
  1 cm (½ inch) dice
4 tablespoons plain flour
50 g (2 oz) Gruyère cheese, grated
1 tablespoon medium dry sherry
1 teaspoon Worcestershire sauce
3 tablespoons finely chopped
  parsley
salt and pepper

1 Heat the oil in a large saucepan, add the bacon and onions and cook over a moderate heat until the onion is pale golden. Add the stock, 600 ml (1 pint) of the measured water and the potatoes. Bring the mixture to the boil, then lower the heat, cover and simmer, for 15 minutes, or until the potatoes are just tender.

2 In a small bowl, whisk the flour with the remaining water and stir it into the soup. Cook, covered, for 5 minutes, stirring frequently.

3 Blend the Gruyère with 300 ml (½ pint) of the soup in a blender or food processor. Stir the purée back into the soup, then add the sherry and Worcestershire sauce with salt and pepper to taste. Simmer for 3–5 minutes, then stir in the parsley just before serving in warmed soup bowls.

Smoked haddock and sweetcorn soup with wild rice and bacon croûtons

serves **4**
preparation time **15 minutes**
cooking time **about 1¼ hours**

75 g (3 oz) wild rice
250 g (8 oz) smoked haddock
600 ml (1 pint) milk
1 bay leaf
50 g (2 oz) butter
1 large onion, chopped
1 leek, sliced
1 celery stick, chopped
1 garlic clove, crushed
1 tablespoon thyme leaves
900 ml (1½ pints) Chicken Stock
   (see page 9)
pinch of grated nutmeg
125 g (4 oz) sweetcorn, defrosted
   if frozen
salt and pepper
2 tablespoons chopped parsley,
   to serve

Bacon croûtons
3 tablespoons olive oil
4 rindless pancetta slices or
   streaky bacon rashers,
   cut into strips
2 slices of bread, crusts removed,
   cut or broken into 1 cm (½ inch)
   pieces

1 Put the rice into a small saucepan and cover with cold water. Bring to the boil, then lower the heat and simmer for 40–45 minutes, or until tender. Drain and set aside.

2 Put the haddock, milk and bay leaf into a saucepan and bring to the boil, then lower the heat and simmer for 8–10 minutes, or until just cooked. Remove the fish with a slotted spoon and leave to cool. Discard the skin and any bones and break the flesh into flakes with a fork. Strain the milk and reserve it.

3 Melt the butter in a large saucepan, add the onion, leek, celery and garlic and cook, without colouring, for 8–10 minutes. Add the thyme, stock and reserved milk. Season with salt, pepper and nutmeg. Bring to the boil, then lower the heat and simmer for 10 minutes. Add the sweetcorn and cook for 5 minutes, then add the rice and flaked haddock and heat for a few minutes. Adjust the seasoning to taste.

4 To make the bacon croûtons, heat the oil in a large frying pan over a moderate heat, add the pancetta or bacon and cook for 5–6 minutes, or until crisp.

5 Remove with a slotted spoon and drain on kitchen paper. Add the bread to the pan and cook for 4–5 minutes, turning frequently, until crisp and golden brown. Drain on kitchen paper.

6 Serve the soup in warmed soup bowls, sprinkled with the bacon croûtons and chopped parsley.

Eight treasure soup

serves **4–6**
preparation time **15–20 minutes**
cooking time **about 15 minutes**

1.2 litres (2 pints) Chicken Stock
(see page 9) or water
50 g (2 oz) frozen peas
50 g (2 oz) frozen sweetcorn
1 small boneless, skinless chicken
breast, about 100 g (3½ oz), cut
into very thin strips
75 g (3 oz) fresh shiitake
mushrooms, stalks removed,
very thinly sliced
3 tablespoons soy sauce,
or to taste
2 tablespoons rice wine or
dry sherry
1 tablespoon cornflour
50 g (2 oz) cooked peeled prawns,
defrosted and dried thoroughly
if frozen
50 g (2 oz) cooked ham, thinly
sliced
150 g (5 oz) firm tofu, drained and
thinly sliced
50 g (2 oz) fresh baby spinach
leaves, very finely shredded
salt and pepper

1 Bring the stock or water to the boil in a large
saucepan. Add the frozen peas and sweetcorn and
simmer for 3 minutes. Add the chicken, mushrooms,
soy sauce and rice wine or sherry. Stir well and simmer
for 3 minutes.

2 Blend the cornflour to a paste with a little cold
water, then pour into the soup and stir to mix. Simmer,
stirring, for 1–2 minutes, or until the soup thickens.

3 Lower the heat to low and add the prawns, ham,
tofu and spinach. Simmer for about 2 minutes, or until
the spinach is just wilted, stirring once or twice. Take
care to stir gently so that the tofu does not break up.
Taste and add salt and pepper if necessary, plus more
soy sauce, if liked. Serve piping hot.

Wheat noodle soup with marinated chicken

serves **4–6**
preparation time **30 minutes**,
plus marinating
cooking time **20–25 minutes**

300 g (10 oz) boneless, skinless
   chicken breasts
1 teaspoon turmeric
2 teaspoons salt
2 lemon grass stalks
3 tablespoons peanuts, skinned
   and roasted
3 tablespoons long-grain
   white rice
2 tablespoons vegetable oil
1 onion, chopped
3 garlic cloves, crushed
5 cm (2 inch) piece of fresh root
   ginger, peeled and finely
   chopped
¼ teaspoon paprika
2 red bird's eye chillies, chopped
2–3 tablespoons Thai fish sauce
900 ml (1½ pints) water
250 g (8 oz) wheat noodles

To serve
3 hard-boiled eggs, halved
2 tablespoons chopped fresh
   coriander leaves
3 spring onions, finely chopped
Thai fish sauce
crushed dried chilli
1–2 tablespoons balachaung
   (optional)

1 Cut the chicken breasts into 2.5 cm (1 inch) cubes.
Mix the turmeric with the salt and rub it into the
cubes of chicken. Cover and leave to stand for
30 minutes.

2 Bruise the lemon grass with the side of a rolling pin
to release the flavour. Finely crush the roasted peanuts
in a food processor or using a pestle and mortar. Heat
a dry frying pan and toast the rice until golden brown,
then finely crush it to a powder in a food processor or
spice grinder.

3 Heat the oil in a large saucepan, add the onion and
cook until just softened. Add the dry marinated chicken
together with the lemon grass, garlic, ginger, paprika
and chillies. Add the fish sauce and measured water
and bring to the boil.

4 Lower the heat and simmer gently. Mix the crushed
peanuts and ground rice and add to the pan. Simmer
for 10–15 minutes, or until the chicken has cooked
through and the broth thickened slightly.

5 Meanwhile, bring a saucepan of water to the boil,
add the noodles and cook for 3–4 minutes, or until just
tender. Drain and refresh with cold water, then divide
between large soup bowls.

6 Ladle the chicken soup over the noodles and serve
topped with hard-boiled eggs, chopped coriander and
spring onions. Add an extra splash of fish sauce and a
sprinkling of crushed dried chilli and balachaung, if
using, to taste. Eat the soup with a spoon and fork.

tip Balachaung is a hot Burmese condiment made
from deep-fried shallots, garlic, chillies and dried
shrimps. You can just use deep-fried shallots, which,
like balachaung, are available from Oriental shops.

Index

Acknowledgements

Executive Editor: Nicky Hill
Senior Editor: Rachel Lawrence
Executive Art Editor: Leigh Jones
Designer: Tony Truscott
Picture Researcher: Luzia Strohmayer
Production Controller: Manjit Sihra

Octopus Publishing Group Limited /Frank Adam 8, 110 /Stephen
Conroy 100–101, 109 /David Loftus 93 /Jeremy Hopley 39 /David
Jordan 73 /Sandra Lane 28, 54, 51–52, 57 /William Lingwood 21 /David
Loftus 2, 22, 50, 69, 94, 97, 99, 118, 125 /Diana Miller 35, 66, 90, 107,
115 /Peter Myers 7, 11, 17, 62 /Sean Myers 32–33, 41, 83, 89 /William
Reavell 24, 43, 45, 82, 85, 111, 113, 119 /Simon Smith 47, 59 /Ian
Wallace 3, 4, 15, 25, 27, 31, 37, 60, 67, 71, 76, 78, 81, 87, 103, 106,
117, 123 /Philip Webb 1, 12–13, 19, 49, 65, 75, 105, 121.

Witch in
the Bush

Witch in the Bush

Madeline Rose

with illustrations by
Trevor Weekes

Angus & Robertson Publishers

ANGUS & ROBERTSON PUBLISHERS

Unit 4, Eden Park, 31 Waterloo Road,
North Ryde, NSW, Australia 2113
and
16 Golden Square, London W1R 4BN, United Kingdom

First published in Australia by Angus & Robertson Publishers in 1985
First published in the UK by Angus & Robertson (UK) Ltd in 1985

Copyright © Madeline Rose 1985

National Library of Australia
Cataloguing-in-publication data.

Rose, Madeline, 1932-
  Witch in the bush.

  For children.
  ISBN 0 207 14997 6.

  I. Weekes, Trevor. II. Title.

A823'.3

Typeset in 12pt Century by Setrite Typesetters
Printed in Hong Kong

CONTENTS

CONTENTS

Amy's Ring

It was fine and warm for the high school sports day.

"Are you coming to watch Jean and Peter?" Mrs Pitt asked the two younger members of the family, who were sprawled on the living-room floor, reading.

"I suppose so," said nine-year-old John, without enthusiasm. "But they never win anything, do they?"

"Not everyone can win," said Mrs Pitt cheerfully. "Our family has never been very good at games. But I'm sure Peter and Jean will try hard and it's up to us to encourage them."

"John is a good runner," said John's twin, Amy. "He won the junior school cup. And I nearly won the high jump. Don't you remember?"

"We all have different talents," said Mrs Pitt. "There's a lot of competition at the high school."

"Are you coming or not?" called Mr Pitt from the hall. "I'm driving off in ten minutes. Anyone who isn't ready will have to walk."

Mrs Pitt hurried away. The twins stayed where they were and considered the question.

1

"We've nothing much else to do," yawned Amy.

They snapped shut their books and slowly followed their parents.

"If we could ride brooms like Granny Enders," whispered John, as they walked down the hall, "we wouldn't need the car."

Amy chuckled. "We could have a special event," she said. "Broomstick racing! That would liven up the school sports."

"I wonder if we'll ever see Granny again?" said John. "It's nearly a whole year since she sailed away on that old broom. I don't suppose she'll come back. When she was tired and weak she needed our help to get from England to Australia. But I don't think she really cared about us. I suppose we're pretty dull company for a witch."

Amy hesitated by the front door. She glanced down at the ring on her finger, the ring Granny Enders had given her when she said goodbye. "I don't know," she said slowly. "Sometimes, lately, I get funny feelings. I look at this stone and I think I see things. I suppose I just imagine them."

"John! Amy! Are you ready?" Jean's voice was urgent. "We're leaving now!"

"Yes, all right. Wait a minute," shouted John, pulling open the door. The others were already in the car; Peter and Jean dressed in shorts, T-shirts and running shoes.

"I think these shoes are getting too small,"

2

said Peter, wriggling his feet, as the car set off down the road. "I'll stub my toes as I run."

"Why didn't you think of that before?" asked his mother in exasperation. "It's too late to do anything about it now."

"I'm sure the elastic in these shorts is giving out," said Jean, tugging dubiously at her waistband.

"If only you'd mentioned it last night!" said Mrs Pitt. She rummaged in her bag and handed Jean a safety pin. "Fasten it with this — just in case."

John did not get a chance to finish his conversation with Amy until they were at the sportsground. He beckoned her away from the others. "What did you mean about the ring?" he asked.

Amy looked embarrassed. "It's probably just my imagination," she said, "but sometimes, not very often, when I look at the stone I think I see little pictures. They only last for a split second, and no matter how long I stare they don't come back."

"What sort of pictures?" asked John, in surprise.

"Different scenes and places," said Amy, frowning. "Places I'm sure I've never seen before. But they're gone before you can look at them properly. Perhaps they're never really there. Perhaps there's something wrong with my eyes."

She pulled off the ring and handed it to John. He stared at the stone. It was clear red and almost transparent, like a piece of coloured glass.

3

But if you tilted it, it shimmered, full of little flickering lights. "I can't see a thing," he said.

"No," said Amy. "Nor can I, usually. It doesn't seem to make sense. The last time was early last week, Tuesday I think. I saw a lonely, sandy plain, almost a desert. At least I think that's what I saw." She slid the ring back on to her finger.

The twins wandered around the outskirts of the oval. The first events were already underway. The sun shone down on the closely clipped grass marked with white lines. Parents and other spectators were seated on rows of benches and chairs, on the north and west sides of the ground. There was a larger crowd than in previous years, as this was the first time the sports had been held on a Saturday.

John and Amy bought ice-blocks from a stall run by the Ladies' Auxiliary, and sat down on the grass to eat them, and to watch the competitors. They did not know many of the high school children, but now and then they recognised some friend of Jean's or Peter's.

Once or twice John saw Amy start and glance down at her hand.

"What's the matter?" he asked.

"The ring," replied Amy. "It keeps making my finger tingle. It's never done that before. If it gets any worse I'll have to take it off."

4

Strange Happenings

As John had foretold, Jean and Peter did not win anything. But neither did they come last in their races. Afterwards they came to sit on the grass next to the twins, to watch the remaining events. John told them about Amy's ring.

"Keep your voice down!" whispered Amy. "Someone else might hear. Do you think I'm imagining it all, Jean?"

"I don't see why you should be," said Jean. "After all the strange things that have happened I wouldn't be a bit surprised to see pictures in a ring."

"How about this tingling?" asked Amy, rubbing her finger.

"You're probably imagining that," said Peter, "because you started puzzling about the pictures."

"Let me wear the ring for a minute," said Jean. "Perhaps I'll see or feel something."

Amy handed it over reluctantly. "Granny Enders told me to wear it all the time," she said.

"It's only for a little while," said Jean, "as an experiment."

She slipped the ring on to her little finger, the only one it fitted, and waited expectantly, staring at the stone. She could see nothing unusual and it certainly didn't make her finger prickle.

"Oh, good!" said Peter presently. "It's time for the high jump."

"Maria will win it," said Jean, raising her eyes from the ring. "There's no-one to touch her."

The children settled down to watch. The girls were first; there were eight of them. At the start they all cleared the rod easily, but as it was moved higher they dropped out one by one.

"Just three left now," said Jean. "Maria, Amanda and Bronwen. Bronwen will be out next. She doesn't usually get as high as this."

Bronwen ran across the smooth grass and leapt into the air. She did not only jump over the bar. She cleared it by at least half a metre. A gasp of astonishment went up from the crowd, followed by furious clapping.

"But she can't jump like that!" exclaimed Jean. "She never could before, anyway."

Next it was Maria's turn, and then Amanda's. They looked unnerved by Bronwen's unexpected success, but they managed the jump. Two teachers stepped forward to move the rod a notch higher.

Bronwen seemed rather dazed. She walked slowly towards the jump, hesitated, then sprang upwards. This time there was a full metre between her heels and the rod. A hush fell over the oval. Then came a wave of applause.

There was really no point in going on. Both Maria and Amanda knew they could never jump as high as that. But they struggled over the next two jumps, before sending the bar tumbling to the ground.

The rod was replaced and Bronwen soared effortlessly over it. She seemed almost to hover for a moment in the air, before landing gracefully on the other side.

"The winner of the girls' high jump is Bronwen Jones," announced the headmistress over the loudspeaker.

The sports master and the headmistress hurried over to the jump and examined it. They called Bronwen over and looked very carefully at her, especially her legs. They asked her to remove her running shoes and they peered inside them.

"What are we looking for?" whispered the headmistress.

"I don't know," said the sports master hoarsely. "But there must be some explanation!"

"Can I go home?" asked Bronwen, looking rather frightened. "I feel a bit sick." She wandered over to the far side of the ground, where her parents pounced on her and bore her proudly away.

"That was amazing!" said Peter. "I wonder how she did it?"

The boys' high jump followed, but "high" proved to be a rather misleading description. Somehow the competitors found it difficult to get off the ground. One by one they ran up to the bar

8

and attempted to jump, but they only managed to rise a few centimetres from the grass. There was a puzzled murmur among the parents.

The sports master strode up to the jump looking furious. "Stop playing the fool!" he stormed. "Who's responsible for this silly performance? We've gone to some trouble to arrange these sports and your parents have come along to support us."

"I'm trying, honestly, Mr Petrov," protested a boy called Carlos, purple-faced with effort. "Something keeps holding me down. I feel as though my feet are made of lead."

The other boys chorused agreement.

"There's something strange about the jump, Mr Petrov," said Carlos.

"The girls had no trouble!" snapped the teacher. "They did extraordinarily well."

On an impulse he ran towards the bar, and attempted to clear it. His feet rose only a fraction from the ground, then he tripped over and fell flat on his face. Before they could stop themselves the children started to laugh. Mr Petrov sat up indignantly, his nose streaming with blood.

"Oh dear!" said the headmistress, hurrying forward with a clean handkerchief. "There's something very wrong here this afternoon. Let's get the rest of the programme over as quickly as possible."

All went smoothly until the last event — a long distance race, six times round the oval. Peter should have been in it, but he had blistered his toe in his small running shoes, so he stayed with his brother and sisters and hoped no one would notice.

There were a good many competitors. They waited tensely for the starting gun, then pounded off along the track. For a while nothing unusual happened. The fastest runners surged ahead and the less able took up their places behind them. They swept round the oval once, then started the second lap.

Suddenly something went wrong for the runners at the front. All of them started to move like people in a slow-motion film. Their arms and legs floated gracefully up and down, like fish in water, or slowly hovering birds. They barely made any headway at all.

Then, as everyone watched incredulously, the runners in the last group began to move very fast. With their legs working like pistons, they shot past all the others and took the lead. The spectators jumped to their feet, shouting with excitement.

But then the fast-running group slowed down, and they in turn began to move with the slow, floating movements of those they had overtaken. And all at once the group at the back started to run rapidly, and surged to the front.

This happened over and over again. At first the parents and teachers shouted, jumped and waved, but presently they fell silent and stared in disbelief. The runners went round and round, speeding up and slowing down, jerking like puppets on strings.

After the sixth circuit they did not stop, but swept on down the track. Mr Petrov ran out ahead of them, waving his arms and shouting, "Stop! Stop! The race is over!"

Just when the sports master thought that the runners were going to trample all over him, they halted abruptly, and fell on top of each other in a great heap.

There was no attempt to decide who had won, and the headmistress was too alarmed to go on to the prizegiving.

"The cups will be presented in Assembly next week," she called over the loudspeaker. "Will you all please go home as quickly and quietly as possible."

"What a shame!" said Amy, glancing over to where the silver trophies glistened on a trestle table, decorated with all the house colours.

There was no wind, and the prefect guarding the prizes did not lay a finger on the table, but suddenly the trophies began to rattle and clash together. The cups danced little jigs and merrily clinked their rims. A wooden shield, studded with little silver plates, thumped up and down on the table top. Someone in the crowd started to scream.

"Please go home," called the headmistress again. "Please go home right away!"

Two teachers ran forward and began to stuff the trophies into a sack. There the prizes lay quite still.

"Well, what did you make of all that?" asked Mr Pitt, as he drove the family back home.

"Extraordinary!" said Mrs Pitt. "I can't remember a sports day like it."

"I'm glad none of it happened to me!" said Jean, with a shiver. "Did you see Rod Sinclair in that last race? His face was purple and he looked really scared."

"Can I have my ring back, Jean?" asked Amy, suddenly remembering.

Jean pulled off the ring and handed it to her sister. "I didn't notice any tingling," she whispered, "and no pictures either."

Amy slipped the ring on to her finger and waited. "It feels all right now," she said.

An Unexpected Visitor

But next day, halfway through the evening meal, Amy's finger began to prickle again. She put down her fork and stared at her hand uneasily. Then the doorbell rang.

"Answer it will you, Peter," said Mr Pitt, helping himself to more vegetables.

Peter opened the front door and blinked. There was no mistaking the figure standing on the step, with the hooked nose, silver hair and glittering eyes. "Granny Enders!" he cried in surprise.

"Well don't just stand there!" growled Mrs Enders. "Aren't you going to ask me in?"

"Yes, of course," mumbled Peter. He stepped aside and she swept past him, her long, green, silky dress billowing in the narrow hall.

"Who was it, Peter?" asked Mr Pitt, turning from the table. Then he saw the figure in the doorway. "Oh, Granny!" he said feebly. "How nice!"

Mrs Enders sat down in Peter's chair and glared around the table. She drummed her knobbly fingers impatiently on the cloth. Rings set with diamonds, rubies and emeralds sparkled

13

above her knuckles. "You might at least have waited dinner for me!" she said.

"But we didn't know you were coming," protested Mrs Pitt nervously. She had only met Granny Enders once before.

"Amy at least should have known," snapped Granny Enders. "Young people these days can't put two and two together."

"Did you know, Amy? Why didn't you tell us?" asked her mother, puzzled.

Amy glanced at the ring on her finger. "I suppose I should have guessed," she murmured.

Mrs Enders seemed suddenly eager to change the subject. She looked cautiously at the dishes on the table. "The usual rubbish, I see," she said. "Perhaps I will have a few carrots."

"Please may I have the rest of *my* dinner?" asked Peter.

Mrs Enders picked up the half-empty plate before her and handed it to him with a grimace of distaste.

Mr Pitt went into the hall to find an extra chair. He made room for Peter next to himself at the head of the table.

"Why are you so cross?" asked John, watching with fascination as Mrs Enders poured mustard over a large mound of carrots. "Last year you said everything was splendid. You said you were getting mellow."

"So I am," said Granny. "Considering the difficulties I have to overcome, and the idiots I have

14

to deal with, I'm as mellow as can possibly be expected."

"Difficulties?" asked Mr Pitt uneasily. "Is there anything we can do, Granny?"

"There's seldom anything *you* can do, George," said Mrs Enders rudely. "When I adopted you, as an orphan, I hoped you would take after my dear friend, your great-grandmother. But having children is a chancy business. It only turns out well every now and again." Her eyes rested on Amy for a brief moment, then she turned back to her carrots.

Mrs Pitt suddenly lost her temper. "I don't know how you can speak to George like that!" she cried. "What do you want, Mrs Enders? You ignore us for a year, then you come here and tell us how useless we are!"

Granny Enders looked taken aback, as though she had been bitten unexpectedly by a small moth. When she spoke again her voice was carefully friendly. "Don't excite yourself, Brenda," she said. "I've come here to do you all a great favour."

"What sort of favour?" asked Mr Pitt suspiciously. He was still annoyed at having been criticised in front of the children.

Mrs Enders finished her carrots and laid her fork neatly across her plate. She sat back in her chair. "I was at the school sports yesterday," she said. "I've never seen such a disgusting exhibition."

15

That explained quite a lot. The children glanced quickly at each other and John kicked Amy under the table.

"There was something very strange about some of the events," said Mrs Pitt.

"I'm not talking about that," said Mrs Enders. "I was watching Jean and Peter, and frankly I was appalled. They have no co-ordination. No stamina at all!"

"We're not as bad as all that!" said Peter indignantly.

"What they need," said Mrs Enders, ignoring him, "is an intensive course of physical culture. It would be a good thing for the twins too. How can this country produce Olympic champions unless we train the young properly? Now, I have a little property out in the bush, with ideal conditions for this sort of project. I'll take the children out there for a few weeks and try to make something of them."

Mr Pitt's mouth had fallen open. He closed it abruptly. "What do you know about sport, Granny?" he stammered. "I never remember you showing the slightest interest in it. When I was a boy you never came to my sports days."

"I know far more about most things than you'll ever know I know," growled Mrs Enders. Then she abruptly changed her expression and smiled sweetly. "How about it, children?" she cooed. "Would you like to come?"

"Yes please!" said Amy and John, Jean and Peter all together. They were doubtful about the physical training, but very excited at the thought of seeing Mrs Enders' new home.

They began to ask question after question. "Where is it, Granny? When can we leave? How shall we get there?"

Mrs Pitt listened to them in amazement. Why the children should want to go off into the bush with this bad-tempered old woman, she could not imagine.

"We'll leave tomorrow morning," said Mrs Enders, ignoring the other questions.

"But we can't," said Jean. "The school term doesn't finish for three weeks."

"Of course you can," said Granny Enders. "Some things are more important than others."

"No, Granny," said Mr Pitt, "I really must put my foot down about this. If the children want to accept your invitation, that's their business. But it must be in the holidays. They can't miss school."

Mrs Enders glared at him and seemed about to say something. Then she paused and smiled. "Well, maybe the day after tomorrow," she said. "No one can say I'm not reasonable."

"Not till the end of term, Granny," said Mrs Pitt firmly.

Mrs Enders rose to her feet. "Things will probably work out," she said. "I shall just have to stay here until they're ready to leave. I'm a little tired. You can prepare my room now, thank you, Brenda!"

"We don't have a spare room," said Mrs Pitt,

in dismay. "Friends usually sleep on the sofa."

Mrs Enders stalked through the door, across the hall and into the living room. She prodded the couch and frowned at the children clustering in the doorway. "I'd like a little peace and quiet now!" she said to them. "I'll see you all in the morning."

Mrs Pitt hurried in with her arms full of sheets and blankets. "Didn't you bring a suitcase, Granny?"

"You don't need bags if you have enough pockets," said Mrs Enders. She reached into the folds of the green dress and pulled out a long, red nightdress.

The children went off into the boys' bedroom to talk.

"What do you make of all that business about sport?" asked Peter suspiciously.

"It's a bit weird," said Jean. "It's not the sort of thing I'd expect her to care about."

"I bet she has some other plan," said John. "I don't think she cares anything about us. She's only come back because she needs some sort of help."

Amy was going to protest, but stopped. Perhaps John was right. "Well, anyway, I want to go, don't you?" she said. "All sorts of interesting things might happen!"

Surprises in the Bathroom

John woke early and wondered why he felt excited. Then he remembered. Granny Enders . . . asleep next door, in the living room! He sat up.

The house was quite silent, except for the birds beginning their morning calls in the garden. John suspected he was the only one awake in the house.

On the other side of the bedroom Peter slept heavily, his nose under the sheets. John tiptoed into the hall. Then he heard an unfamiliar sound, a rhythmical droning, rising and falling. He peeped round the living room door.

Granny Enders was snoring, her silver curls propped against a blue velvet cushion. She looked older when she was asleep. She had not removed her rings before going to bed and the hand clutching the edge of the sheet sparkled and shone in a shaft of light streaming between the curtains.

John went to the bathroom to wash his hands and face. He was soaping his fingers when he suddenly noticed two unfamiliar objects. On the

19

ledge behind the basin were a small tube with a screw top and a cake of rainbow-coloured soap.

I suppose that's Granny's toothpaste, thought John. He unscrewed the top of the tube and peered inside. If it was toothpaste, it was a strange colour — a brilliant green. John put the tube down again and, as usual, he forgot to replace the cap.

He turned his attention to the soap. The rainbow colours intrigued him. Were they just on the surface, or did they swirl right through the cake? What colour would the suds be?

John listened for a moment. The house was still quiet. He picked up the soap, dipped it in the basin and lathered it between his hands. The foam was disappointingly white and ordinary.

I've already washed my hands once, thought John. So he rubbed the suds all over his face. He stood for a minute, making faces at himself in the mirror through the thick froth. Then he rinsed away the soap and dried his hands and face on a towel.

He was just turning to leave the bathroom, when he suddenly caught a glimpse of himself in the mirror.

His face had turned blue! He glanced down at his hands. The palms were also blue. His startled yell woke everyone in the house — except Mrs Enders, who continued to snore peacefully.

"It won't wash off!" cried Mrs Pitt despairingly, as she scrubbed John's cheeks. "We shall have to ask Granny Enders what to do. I'll wake her with a nice hot cup of tea."

Mrs Enders leant on the arm of the couch and sipped the tea, wearing a sour expression. "That soap is specially formulated for my particular skin. Of course John's face has turned blue! What else did he expect?"

"But will it stay blue?" asked John anxiously.

"I shouldn't think so," said Mrs Enders. "A pity! In a few hours you should be back to your own uninteresting colour."

A startled shriek split the air. They all rushed to see what had happened. Jean was standing in the doorway of the bathroom, looking incredulously at the tiled floor. At first glance it seemed to be covered with writhing green snakes. Then they saw that it was just one snake — a toothpaste snake, pouring from the tube John had left on the ledge. It streamed to the floor, then wound over the tiles in seemingly endless green coils.

Mrs Enders pushed roughly past Jean, strode through the mess and screwed the top firmly back on the tube.

"I will not have this meddling with my personal belongings!" she snapped. "George, you have made an appalling job of bringing up these children! I can see I shall have to stay in touch, to keep an eye on them. It's disgraceful!"

"I only left the top off the toothpaste," protested John. "Nothing happens when I leave the top off ours." He accepted a bucket and mop from

21

his mother and gloomily began to clean the bathroom floor.

Mrs Enders was back on the sofa, finishing her cup of tea. "How did all that toothpaste fit into that tiny tube?" asked Peter. But he didn't get an answer.

"I've had a very bad night," said Mrs Enders. "This couch is most uncomfortable. I haven't had a wink of sleep."

"Are you sure, Granny?" asked Mr Pitt, collecting her empty cup. "We thought we heard you snoring."

"Snoring?" repeated Mrs Enders, in a frosty and terrible voice. "Your ears are as useless as the rest of you, George. You heard the blinds rattling, or the woodwork creaking. Snoring indeed! I haven't closed my eyes. I'm black and blue."

"Oh dear," said Mrs Pitt. "I thought the couch was quite comfortable. No one has ever complained before. I must see if I can pad it with a quilt."

"A lot of good that will do!" said Mrs Enders.

Granny Makes Herself Comfortable

After breakfast Mr Pitt went off to his office. Mrs Pitt had to go shopping.

"Hurry up and get ready for school," she said to the children. "You're going to be late."

"I can't go to school with a blue face," objected John.

"Of course he can't," said Mrs Enders, appearing at the kitchen door. "And besides, I need the children here to look after me while you're out. I'm feeling very sick and frail."

Mrs Pitt looked at Granny Enders suspiciously. She seemed the picture of health. Her cheeks were pink, her eyes glittered. "You don't look sick!" said Mrs Pitt.

"I don't think you realise how very old I am," said Mrs Enders. "Extremely old people need to be cared for. They shouldn't be neglected and left to fend for themselves. Here I am, a poor, weak, old woman! I've travelled hundreds of kilometres to see my dear grandchildren, and what reward do I get? I'm to be left alone, in an empty house!"

Mrs Pitt felt she really could not cope with Granny Enders just then.

23

"Well, maybe. Just for this morning," she said unwillingly. She called the children into her bedroom. "Granny is a guest," she said. "I know she's difficult, but we must be nice to her. See she has everything she wants."

No sooner had Mrs Pitt left to do her shopping than Mrs Enders called the children into the living room. "There's something I should like to do," she said, "before your dear mother gets back."

Jean looked at her uneasily. Mrs Enders was perched at one end of the despised sofa, with a dangerous glitter in her eye. She was wearing a voluminous dress of brilliant purple, appliquéd with silver stars. A high purple frill surrounded her skinny neck.

That dress must have come from a pocket in last night's green dress, thought Jean. Just like the nightdress and the soap and the toothpaste. They must be enormous pockets! And where are the green dress and the nightdress now? In the pockets of the purple dress? She shook her head. It felt muddled.

"I hope you have a street directory," said Mrs Enders. "Ah! Good, Amy, I see you are wearing your ring. Come over here and sit by me."

Peter fetched the directory from its place by the telephone in the hall. Amy settled herself on the sofa, pleasantly excited. She thought Granny Enders' dress was beautiful. The stars shone so brightly that she was sure they would glow even in the dark.

"Now, silence, everyone!" said Mrs Enders. "I have to concentrate." She leaned back and closed her eyes with a fierce frown. For five minutes nothing happened, then she suddenly exclaimed, "That will do!"

"What will?" asked John.

"Look in the ring, Amy," said Mrs Enders, still with her eyes tightly shut. "What do you see?"

Amy gazed at the ring. For a moment she saw only the transparent, red stone. Then it clouded briefly and cleared to a tiny picture. The picture wavered and vanished.

"It's gone!" said Amy. "Something was there, but it's gone."

"You need practice," said Mrs Enders, screwing up her eyelids. "Try harder!"

"I don't know how," said Amy, but she stared at the stone and the little picture came back, wobbly, but fairly clear.

"What do you see?" asked Mrs Enders.

"A van," said Amy. "A big one."

John craned over his twin's shoulder. He could see nothing in the limpid depths of the red jewel.

"Now, where is it?" asked Mrs Enders urgently. "I don't know this district at all. Can you see a street sign, or a shop you recognise?"

Amy bent closer over the ring. "I think it's at the traffic lights in the middle of Fingham Street. Yes, I can see the post office."

"Good girl!" exclaimed Mrs Enders, opening her eyes. "Now, quickly, Peter. Don't just stand there! Find that place in the directory for me."

Peter fumbled with the pages. "It's right here."

"And where is this house?" asked Mrs Enders.

"Oh, we're over on the next map," said Peter,

turning the page of the directory and pointing.

"Bother!" snapped the old woman. "Well, it can't be helped." She flicked back the page to the first map, then hunched over it. She began tracing the road with a bony, bejewelled finger.

Amy looked hard at her ring, but the picture had vanished. Try as she might, she could not bring it back.

Slowly Granny's finger travelled across the page. The children didn't know what to expect, but they stayed quiet, hardly daring to breathe.

The finger reached the margin and jumped swiftly round on to the following page. Slowly it crept along the wavy line of the road where they lived. Then Mrs Enders sat back with a satisfied smile. She seemed to be listening. Suddenly the doorbell rang, and the children jumped.

"Well, answer it!" said Mrs Enders. "Don't just sit there like a row of puddings!"

Peter was the first down the hall. He opened the door. The path was blocked by something enormous, supported by two dazed-looking men in overalls. The nearer one spoke.

"One king-size waterbed," he said in a flat, singsong voice. "Special delivery."

"It must be a mistake," said Peter.

"It can't be for us," said Jean.

"Nonsense," grunted Mrs Enders, pushing the children out of the way. "Everything's quite correct. In here with it, if you please!"

The men moved very slowly and had a strange, dreamy look about them, but they managed to manoeuvre the huge frame down the hall. They set it right in the middle of the living room floor. The rest of the furniture was squashed against the walls.

"What are Mum and Dad going to say?" muttered Peter, as they watched the men fit the mattress and fill it with water from a hose.

"They can hardly complain," said Mrs Enders. "I distinctly heard your mother tell you I was to have anything I wanted."

When Mrs Pitt came home, she was flabbergasted. "What a terrible mistake! Surely you must have realised it was a wrong delivery!" she said.

"Unhappily, no," said Mrs Enders. "I thought you had planned a nice surprise, to make me comfortable, after that dreadful night on your lumpy sofa."

"But you must see that this won't do, Granny! There's no room to move in here. It will have to go back right away."

"We can't send it back," said Mrs Enders, with a sunny smile. "We don't know where it came from."

"What do you mean, you don't know?" exclaimed Mrs Pitt. "Wasn't there a delivery docket?"

"No," said Jean. "They didn't seem to think about that."

"But didn't one of you notice the name on the van?"

"No," said the children truthfully. They had

been so intrigued by the bed itself that it had never occurred to them to go out and look at the van.

"Since the bed is here," said Mrs Enders, "we shall keep it. Don't fuss, Brenda. I know George would want me to be comfortable!"

Mrs Pitt went into the hall to phone her husband. "Granny insists on keeping the thing. What will I do?" she pleaded.

"Take no notice," said Mr Pitt firmly, brave in the security of his office. "Goodness, Brenda, you can surely manage one old woman!"

"She's your grandmother," said Mrs Pitt crossly. 'Why don't you come home and manage her yourself?"

"She's not my real grandmother, as well you know!" shouted Mr Pitt. Then he saw his secretary looking surprised, and pulled himself together. "Phone all the furniture shops, dear. Someone's bound to be missing a waterbed."

Mrs Pitt sat down with the telephone directory. She made a long, long list of all the shops that might possibly sell waterbeds. Then she rang the first number.

"This is a recorded message," said a woman's voice. "This shop is closed today for the annual furniture retailers' picnic."

"Bother!" said Mrs Pitt. She phoned the second number on her list. This time it was a man's voice, but it said the same thing.

"This shop is closed today for the annual furniture retailers' picnic."

The third call was the same, and the fourth, and the fifth, and the sixth and the seventh.

"It's no good, dear, is it?" called Mrs Enders, reclining on the waterbed, propped on a pile of cushions. "Why don't you give up and make us all some lunch?"

"Somewhere must be open!" said Mrs Pitt wildly. "Those delivery men weren't at the picnic. If only I could hit on the right number! There's something very peculiar about all these recorded messages. They all use exactly the same words."

"Just lack of imagination," said Mrs Enders. "It's the way people are educated today. I blame the schools."

An hour later Mrs Pitt did give up. She was so frazzled that she forgot to send the children off to school in the afternoon. When Mr Pitt arrived home in the evening the waterbed still filled the living room and the children were sprawled across it, around Mrs Enders, happily watching television.

"I'm sure Granny Enders arranged the whole thing," said Mrs Pitt to her husband. "Well, I've done my best. It's up to you to put your foot down, George."

"I'll have it out with her now," soothed Mr Pitt. He strode into what was left of the living room.

"Now what's going on, Granny?" he said briskly.

Mrs Enders gave him a terrible glare. "Be

quiet, George! You're interrupting the programme."

"What about this bed?" raged Mr Pitt.

"It's only for tonight," said Mrs Enders
calmly. "I'll be leaving in the morning with the
children!"

"The children can't go till school finishes,"
shouted Mr Pitt. "Brenda had no right to keep
them at home today. That's my last word!"

"Do relax, George," said Mrs Enders, settling
back on her cushions. "Things have a way of
working themselves out."

Mr Pitt went back to the kitchen. "I made
myself quite clear," he said to his wife. "She can't
push me around. I'm not a little boy any more."

An Unusual Car

"Good grief!" said Peter next morning, looking out of the bedroom window. "There's a very strange car outside our gate. Come and look, John! Whatever is it?"

John, who was only half awake, stumbled over the floor and stared through the glass. An old-fashioned looking car, with polished brass fittings, stood by the kerb. The body was high, squarish and purple. The mud-guards were enormous.

"It must be a vintage car," said John sleepily.

"It's not like any of the pictures I've seen," said Peter. "I'm going out to get a better look." He pulled on his dressing-gown and ran out of the house, with John close behind him. Jean and Amy joined them a few moments later.

Peter prowled round and round the car. "There's no manufacturer's name, no numbers or anything," he said.

"It looks like a homemade car to me," said Jean. "Someone has collected a lot of little bits and stuck them all together. Nothing quite matches."

"I think it's lovely," sighed Amy, fingering a gleaming brass lamp by the driver's seat. "Look at those seats . . . red velvet, all padded and cushiony."

The horn was a long, cornet shape, with a soft rubber bulb to squeeze. John leaned forward and squeezed it, but it made no sound at all.

"Don't, John!" said Jean. "The owner might be cross. I wonder whose it is? It wasn't here yesterday."

They went back into the house. In the kitchen they found Granny Enders consuming a pile of toast. She was wearing yet another dress, a vast tent patterned with swirls of black and orange. In between mouthfuls she was explaining to Mrs Pitt exactly what was wrong with her homemade marmalade.

"You don't like jam anyway!" Mrs Pitt said crossly. "I remember George telling me so quite clearly."

"Marmalade is not jam," Mrs Enders stated, raising an eyebrow in a superior manner.

"Of course it is!" insisted Mrs Pitt. "It's just a jam made with oranges. You boil up the fruit with sugar and water in exactly the same way."

"I wonder," said Mrs Enders, with a withering smile, "if you can tell the difference between a turnip and a forget-me-not?"

Mrs Pitt stared at her.

"In both cases," said Granny Enders, "you plant a seed in the soil, and you water it. The results, however, are rather different."

She turned to the children. "How do you like my car?" she asked in a self-satisfied tone.

"It's beautiful!" exclaimed Amy.

"*Your* car?" cried John.

"It's very unusual," said Peter. "What make is it?"

"Nothing that you would know," replied Granny Enders.

"How did it get here? Who brought it?" asked Jean. But the old woman munched her toast and did not reply.

"By the look of it, it will probably use a lot of petrol," said Mrs Pitt, annoyed about the marmalade.

"Oh dear me, no!" said Mrs Enders, smiling. "It's very economical!"

"The horn doesn't work," said John.

"Nonsense," sniffed Granny Enders. "Of course it does! Now off you all go, and pack your bags."

"Don't do anything of the sort," cried Mrs Pitt. "You know what your father said, and I fully agree. You have to finish school before you go on holiday."

"I should pack your things just the same," said Mrs Enders, setting down her coffee cup with a clang. "It's best to be prepared."

The kitchen door suddenly opened, and Mr Pitt stood there in his dressing-gown, his face covered with shaving foam. He waved a squawking transistor radio at them. "I've been listening to the local news," he said. "There's a big outbreak of measles. They're closing the schools for the rest of the term, to stop it spreading."

"How very convenient!" said Mrs Enders. "I told you things would sort themselves out. No need for us to argue now, Brenda. Off you go, children. Hurry up!"

"Wait a minute . . . " began Mr Pitt, and then he stopped. He somehow couldn't think of any reason why the children shouldn't leave. He felt rather strange, and passed a hand over his eyes.

"Can't we have some breakfast first?" asked Peter, hungrily eyeing the piece of toast in Granny Enders' hand.

"I'm starving!" complained John.

"Oh, very well, I suppose so," said Mrs Enders peevishly, taking another bite. "Children these days seem to think of nothing but their stomachs."

An hour later they loaded their cases into the boot, and climbed into the huge old car. Mrs Enders of course had no luggage at all. Their parents stood on the kerb, looking baffled, like people just waking from a dream.

"Wait . . . what if they come down with measles while they're away?" asked Mr Pitt.

"They won't," said Granny Enders. "I guarantee it."

"Where are you going? Where do you live?" asked Mrs Pitt, looking confused. "How can we get in touch with you?"

"So sorry, Brenda," said Mrs Enders, leaning

out of the window, "I never can remember addresses. I'll let you know, when I have the chance to look it up."

They drove away. Mrs Pitt's voice grew fainter behind them. "How can you find anywhere," she cried, "if you don't even know the address?"

Amy was in the front seat, next to Granny Enders, and the three other children sat in the back. Jean couldn't help feeling guilty. They were driving away with Mrs Enders, happy and

excited, while their friends lay in bed. Measles could be very unpleasant, too. "It's not really fair," she said unhappily. "All those people getting sick..."

"What has fairness got to do with it?" queried Mrs Enders, spinning the wheel.

"Well, you did it, didn't you?" asked Peter. "You gave them all measles!"

"I gave them no such thing," said Granny Enders.

"Well it was strange that it happened like

that," said Peter. "Just when we wanted to get away."

Mrs Enders swung the car into the thick of the traffic. "It may not be measles after all," she said. "One spot looks very like another."

"Will they get better soon?" asked Amy anxiously.

"How should I know?" said Mrs Enders. "What has it to do with me? But I wouldn't be a bit surprised. If I had to guess, I would say their spots are disappearing just about now."

It was a fine morning with a misty sky. The car bowled smoothly along the street.

"Did you ever hear such a quiet engine?" marvelled Peter.

They all strained their ears. There was a slight hissing noise, which might have been the tyres on the road, but they could hear none of the familiar noises of their family car. In fact, this car was so silent that no one heard it coming. Several times Mrs Enders had to sound the old-fashioned horn, to make pedestrians jump out of the way. The horn, which had refused to work for John, made a loud, blaring noise when she squeezed the rubber bulb.

"People are staring at us," said John, waving to a small boy on a bicycle. "They've never seen a car like this before!"

Jean started worrying about Mrs Enders forgetting her own address. She was after all very, very old. It was only by treating herself with special herbs, herbs that she had come to

Australia to find, that she stayed so active. What if they should all get lost, out in the bush? "Which way are we going, Granny?" she asked.

"West," said Mrs Enders crisply, taking them round a corner at an incredible speed.

Jean shut her eyes. When she opened them she was relieved to see they were still on the road.

"Have you really forgotten your address?" asked John curiously.

Mrs Enders twisted round and glared at him. "Are you suggesting I wasn't telling your mother the truth?"

"Er . . . no . . . of course not," answered John. The car swerved wildly, and Mrs Enders turned her attention back to the wheel.

The children would have liked to ask more questions. They were longing to discuss things among themselves, but Granny Enders seemed to be in a touchy mood. It was difficult to talk freely while she sat there straight and stiff, her bony, beringed fingers clenching the wheel and her glittering eyes focused on the road ahead.

All day they drove. At lunchtime Mrs Enders handed round cartons of milk and little bags of something that looked like bird-seed, but tasted rather better.

"I'd much rather have had a meat pie," whispered Peter to Jean.

Mrs Enders did not eat anything herself, but drove on with grim concentration. The further they went, the wilder her driving became. They were out of the city now and the road was edged

39

with soft shoulders of red dirt. Past sun-bleached paddocks and through belts of gum trees they drove, faster and faster. Fortunately there were few other cars on the road. They climbed into the mountains and rushed down to the plains on the other side. Finally, in the evening, they pulled up outside a lonely motel.

Dinner for Six

In spite of the car's comfortable seats, the children were stiff and weary. They had had no chance to use their legs since setting out that morning. They wandered around, stretching and groaning. It was dusk and the breeze was pleasantly cool.

"Come along! It's already arranged. Unit number seven," said Mrs Enders briskly.

Unit seven was a family suite, with beds for four.

"But there are five of us," protested Peter.

"I shall be in the car," said Granny Enders.

"You won't be comfortable there!" cried Amy. "Have my bed. I'll sleep in the car."

"Out of the question," snapped the old woman.

"But Granny, you couldn't sleep properly on the sofa. In the car you won't even be able to lie down!"

"Kindly mind your own business," growled Mrs Enders. "And stop trying to order me around. Where is the menu for room service?"

They found the menu in a plastic folder on the

41

dressing-table, and pored happily over the choice of dishes. After the bird-seed lunch they were all very hungry.

"Choose something everyone likes," said Mrs Enders. "Just one main dish, please, and one dessert."

"Chicken," said Amy.

"Fish," said Jean.

"Why can't we all have different things?" asked Peter.

"One dish only," said Mrs Enders in a stern and terrible voice. "Life is difficult enough without wilfully adding complications."

In the end they all agreed to have steak and salad and apple pie.

Mrs Enders picked up the phone. "Room service please," she said. "May I have dinner for one, in unit seven? Steak and salad and apple pie."

She replaced the receiver. The children looked at her in dismay.

"Dinner for one?" said Jean. "But that won't be nearly enough!"

The corner of Mrs Enders' mouth twitched into a smile. "They are very generous with their helpings in these places," she said. "I shall have a bath while we're waiting for the meal. Amuse yourselves quietly." She swept into the bathroom and locked the door.

There was little chance of being overheard above the noise of rushing water.

"I want to go home," moaned John. "She's a mean old thing, feeding us on bird-seed, and buying one dinner between five people."

"I'm ravenous," said Peter. "Could we buy anything ourselves? I've got two dollars. How much have you, Jean?"

"Nothing," replied Jean. "We left in such a hurry, I forgot about money."

John had forty cents. Amy had five cents.

"Less than three dollars altogether," said Jean. "Not enough to buy extra meals here. But if we could find a little shop, it might go quite a long way."

"There are no shops," said Amy, gazing out of the window into the gathering darkness. "Just trees."

"We'll have to have a straight talk with Granny Enders," said Peter. "We're supposed to be staying with her for quite a while. We can't go on like this!"

But Mrs Enders spent a long time in the bathroom, and just as she emerged, fully dressed once more and pink-cheeked from the steam, there was a knock on the door.

"Dinner for one," said a woman in an apron, looking into the crowded room in surprise.

"Thank you," said Mrs Enders, taking the tray.

"Will you please leave the tray outside, when you've finished," said the woman.

"Remember that, children," said Mrs Enders.

She placed the tray on a low coffee-table by the window. The big plate had a silvery cover, to keep the food hot. The salad was arranged in a little wooden bowl. The tray also held cutlery, salt and pepper and a paper napkin.

It smells good, thought Amy. I'm terribly hungry. I wonder how much there will be?

"Now all quickly into the bathroom and wash your hands!" ordered Mrs Enders.

"We'll have to eat with our fingers," said Jean. "There's only one knife and fork."

They came out of the bathroom and stared in surprise. On the low table six trays were stacked, one on top of the other.

"You were playing a joke on us, Granny!" cried Amy. "You've ordered some more! And there's one tray too many!"

"How did they cook it and bring it so quickly?" asked Jean, mystified.

"It's been a long, hard day," yawned Mrs Enders. "I shall have my meal in peace and privacy." She picked up the top two trays and walked towards the door.

"Why do you need two?" asked John, recovering from his surprise.

"Mind your own business!" said Mrs Enders crossly. "Open the door for me. Now don't let me hear anything more from you till morning."

"I don't understand this," said Peter, when they were alone. "There just wasn't time."

They took off the covers and looked at the food. The helpings were identical.

"Look," said Jean. "The steaks are exactly the same shape and size, browned in just the same way."

44

"Even the chips match," said John. "See that funny-shaped one? There's one on every plate!"

The side salads too were the same, fluting their uniform lettuce leaves round unvarying tomato and cucumber rings.

"Let's eat it all quickly," said Amy. "It might disappear again!"

Next morning, as Granny Enders was starting the car, a woman came running from the office with a worried frown. She was carrying a slip of paper. "Excuse me," she said, "I'm the manager. There seems to be some discrepancy in our accounts."

"How unfortunate!" said Mrs Enders icily. "What has that to do with us?"

The manager looked extremely embarrassed. "Only one meal is listed for your unit last night," she said, "but one of the kitchen-hands happened to remark that she collected six trays from outside your door. Someone must have made a mistake."

Mrs Enders seemed to swell with fury. "If you leave trays around all over the place, that's your business!" she snapped.

Now the manager started to get angry. The children shrank back in their seats and watched, fascinated, as the two women glared at each other through the car window.

"If there were six trays," said the manager, "then there must have been six meals."

"Do you keep no records of your foodstuffs?"

45

demanded Mrs Enders. "Do you buy steaks without counting them? Go back to your kitchen my good woman, and check your supplies! No wonder the tourist industry is in such a state, if it's run by such incompetents! I should count your trays too. I shall wait here for your apology. Now run along! My time is valuable."

The manager looked so taken aback, and then so enraged, that John thought for a moment that she would hit Mrs Enders. But she managed to contain herself and turned sharply on her heel.

"That wasn't really fair," whispered Peter.

"Nonsense," replied Mrs Enders. "I can't stand ingratitude! We not only bring this woman valuable custom, we increase her equipment. She now has five extra tray settings. But instead of thanks we get only abuse!"

"But she doesn't understand," said Jean, wondering if she did either.

"Ignorance," said Mrs Enders, "is no excuse and never has been."

It was a subdued manager who finally came back to the car. "There seems to have been some confusion," she said. "I'm sorry to have caused you any inconvenience."

"Don't let it happen again!" said Granny Enders grimly. She drove off with a jerk that threw the children back in their seats.

Another Reunion

They had been travelling for a little while when
something occurred to Peter. "Granny," he said,
"this car's fuel consumption is fantastic! We
drove all yesterday, and never stopped at a
garage. But the petrol must be running low by
now."

"Oh no," replied Mrs Enders. "As I told your
mother, it's very economical."

Peter was silent for a moment. "No car is as
cheap to run as that!" he muttered to the others.
"Especially not one this size."

John leaned over Mrs Enders. "Which is the
fuel gauge?" he asked with interest.

"It doesn't have one," said Mrs Enders. "It
isn't necessary. Stop sticking your chin in my
shoulder."

The children looked at each other and
wondered. It would not be very pleasant to run
out of fuel, far from anywhere.

Just about then they came in sight of a
garage. It was a small weatherboard affair with
two lonely pumps and a large notice — LAST

PETROL FOR TWO HUNDRED KILO-
METRES. A man in overalls was hosing down
the concrete.

"Fill her up?" he asked, as Mrs Enders
brought the car to a halt.

"No, thank you," said Mrs Enders primly. "I
should just like to use your rest room."

"Well such as it is," grinned the man, "it's
round the back."

Mrs Enders disappeared behind the low,
wooden shack. The garage man looked dubiously
at the car and at the road ahead.

"People usually fill up here," he said to the
children. "Plenty in the tank, have you?"

"We don't see how we can have," said Jean,
looking worried. "Perhaps we could buy a bit
ourselves. How much petrol do you get for two
dollars, forty-five?"

"Not very much these days," said the man.
"Let's just check how much you have." He stuck
his head and hand through the window, then
paused, staring at the dashboard. "Where's the
fuel gauge?" he asked.

"She said there isn't one," replied Peter.

Jean was watching anxiously for Granny
Enders' return. "Just give us as much petrol as
you can," she said hastily. "Hand over your
money, everyone! It may stop us breaking down."

The garage man walked round the car, then
came back to the window. "I can't seem to find
the intake," he muttered, looking puzzled. "Do
you know where it is?"

The children climbed out of the car and helped him to look, but there seemed to be nowhere to pump in the petrol.

"This is the weirdest car I've ever set eyes on," said the man. "Let me just have a look at the engine."

He grasped two little brass handles and lifted up the bonnet. Then he staggered back.

"Good grief!" he yelled.

The children just stood and stared. There was no engine at all in the car. The cavity where the engine should have been was lined with thick red carpet, and on the carpet sprawled a Siamese cat.

"Candar!" gasped the children.

Candar stared at them coolly. He looked sleek and well-fed — just the same as on the day he'd flown out of their lives with Granny Enders nearly a year ago.

"Candar!" cried Amy again. "How are you? Where have you been?"

The cat did not reply. He spat viciously at the garage man and slashed his claws very close to his nose. The man jumped back and slammed down the bonnet.

"I don't remember asking you to meddle with my vehicle!" The cold voice of Granny Enders froze the air. She moved towards the white-faced man. "Kindly get out of my way! Into the car, children! Hurry up now!"

The garage man backed slowly away, looking dumbfounded. He stared after the departing car for a very long time.

"That's why you took two dinners last night!" said John.

"Why didn't you tell us about Candar?" asked Amy happily.

"This sort of driving," said Mrs Enders, "requires intense concentration. Don't pester me with needless questions."

They drove and they drove. For lunch and for dinner they had more milk and "bird-seed". After the second meal, Mrs Enders stopped the car and let them get out to stretch their legs. It was growing dark and there was nothing in sight but a vast expanse of low scrub. The dirt road ran far ahead into the dusk.

"Where are we now? Where are we stopping tonight?" asked Jean, yawning.

"We're not stopping tonight," said Mrs Enders. "You can sleep in the car."

"We'll never manage to sleep," grumbled Peter.

But they did. After the brief exercise, the velvet seats seemed very comfortable. The children lay back and watched shrubs and stunted trees rushing past them, illuminated briefly by the car headlights. Above them the dark sky was thick with stars. Slowly they drifted, first into a pleasant doze, then into a deep sleep.

Once during the night Amy opened her eyes and looked drowsily around. Peter and John were sprawled beside her. Jean's head lolled on the seat in front. Mrs Enders sat stiff and upright at the

wheel, her silver hair glowing slightly in the dark. Something was different, and Amy suddenly realised what it was. Before she had fallen asleep, the car had been bumping and jolting over the rough, stony road. Now it ran so smoothly that it might have been on a city street.

Amy sat up and glanced out of the window. Then she gave a soft little gasp and clutched the edge of the seat. The ground was further away than usual. The car was skimming smoothly along, about a metre above the road.

"Shhh, you're dreaming. Go back to sleep, Amy," whispered Granny Enders.

Granny Enders' Problem

When the children woke next morning, the car was standing on a rough dirt track. On every side stretched a vast, sandy plain, with patches of spinifex and low, thorny vegetation. Far, far away, half hidden in a morning haze, were mountains.

The travellers climbed stiffly out of the car. By the side of the track, in front of a big thorny bush, was a square wooden post. On top of the post was nailed a tin drum, with 'ENDERS' painted upon it. "My mailbox," said Granny Enders. She poked her hand into the drum and pulled out two envelopes, which she stuffed into her pocket.

"The address!" said Jean. "It must be on those letters."

"Of course it is," said Mrs Enders. "How else would they have got here?"

"What is it?" asked Peter. "You couldn't remember when Mum asked you."

The old woman patted her pocket and glared at him. "Why should you need to know the address? You're already here!"

"We could send it to Mum," began Jean, but Mrs Enders did not seem to be listening. She turned back to the car and opened the door.

"Look at this!" shouted John suddenly. He scrabbled in the bush behind the mailbox and pulled out a long, green broom. "However did this get here? Is it yours, Granny?"

"Put that back where you found it, you meddlesome child!" cried Mrs Enders. "You must not interfere with my arrangements. I won't have it! Push that well down, where no one will see it."

"I didn't know I was interfering," muttered John. Crossly he poked the broom handle right below the thorny branches. Whoever pulled it out again was going to get scratched.

They climbed back into their seats and Granny Enders turned the car off the track and headed very fast towards the mountains. The car ran surprisingly smoothly over the bumpy ground. Amy suspected that they were skimming just above the surface. She craned her neck to look, but the big, old-fashioned mudguards hid the wheels.

They drove for an hour or so.

"You live a long way from your mail box," said John at last.

"I live a long way from most things," replied Mrs Enders.

A few minutes later, the car stopped by a small, shabby weatherboard house with a sagging roof and broad verandahs. A dry creek bed ran nearby and the plain stretched on all sides. The mountains seemed as far away as ever.

"Gosh it's hot!" said Jean, as they stepped out of the car.

"Everything's all dried up," said Peter. "All cracked."

And there were indeed cracks everywhere — in the ground under their feet, in the dry creek bed, in the unpainted wooden walls of the little building.

"Why would anyone build a house in a place like this?" asked John.

"Someone tried to farm here once," said Mrs Enders. "Someone somewhat foolhardy. Still, they saved me a lot of trouble."

"I wonder how Candar is?" said Amy, rushing to open the car bonnet. The little cat looked up and yawned, then leapt lightly out of the carpeted cavity and up on to the verandah.

He spoke in the same thin, high voice the children remembered. "I don't expect thanks," he said, "but a little gratitude would be pleasant."

"We are all most grateful, Candar," said Mrs Enders politely. "You have been very helpful."

The children followed Granny Enders out of the glare of the sun, through the front door of the small house. There they stood and stared in surprise. Under their feet was a soft tangerine carpet. There were deep easy chairs, upholstered in cream brocade. The dining table was a carved, polished antique. Over their heads whirred a huge circular fan, wafting cool air to every corner of the room. It was hard to believe after stepping from the harsh desert outside.

Mrs Enders' ill humour seemed to have vanished. She sighed happily and sank down into one of her armchairs. Candar jumped on to her knee.

"I'm tired after all that driving," said Mrs Enders. "Go through there all of you and make us some breakfast."

The kitchen was even more amazing, with its gleaming cupboards and bench-tops.

"Look at this marvellous stove!" said Amy.

"Gosh, she's even got a dishwasher," said John.

In one corner a large refrigerator hummed softly to itself, and the freezer next to it turned out to be packed on every shelf with vegetables and fruit.

"What can we have for breakfast?" wondered Jean, very confused.

The inside of the house looked so different to the outside she felt the solid things around her might suddenly vanish.

"There are eggs in the fridge," said Peter. "Let's boil some."

He took a saucepan to the sink. "That's funny," he said. "The taps don't work."

The others came to look. Jean hesitantly opened the living-room door. "There's no water in the taps, Granny."

"Of course there isn't!" replied Mrs Enders grimly, from her armchair. "That's just the trouble. There should be some in the tank round the back. But don't waste it. It may have to last us a while."

The children went outside. It was hotter and drier and dustier than ever. Behind the house they found an old galvanised tank, with a pipe leading from the gutter round the rusty iron roof. Peter tapped the tank at various levels. Most of it sounded hollow and empty. The water he drained into the pan from a tap at the bottom of the tank had a brownish tinge.

Jean also filled the electric jug. "The tea will probably taste funny," she said.

They trailed back into the house, carrying the precious water carefully.

While Amy timed the eggs, bobbing in their saucepan on the stove, and John toasted sliced, frozen bread, Peter prowled round the outside of the building. After a while he came back into the kitchen and peered behind the fridge and the dishwasher.

"What are you looking for?" asked Jean, busily laying the table.

"I couldn't find a generator anywhere," said Peter. "All the power points seem to work, and she must use lots of juice with all these gadgets. But where does the electricity come from?"

"She makes it herself," said Amy dreamily, fishing the eggs from the saucepan with a table-spoon. "She can do anything now. Anything at all!"

"No I can't," said Mrs Enders flatly, from the

doorway. "And that's why you're here." She sat down at the kitchen table and helped herself to a slice of toast.

"What about our 'intensive course of physical culture'?" asked John suspiciously. "What about all the Olympic training you were going to give us?"

"Oh, that!" said Mrs Enders, looking mildly surprised. "Well, who knows? Perhaps later on. Pass me the marmalade, please! Now, this is real marmalade. Not like the stuff your mother makes."

"Well, that's a relief!" said Peter. "I'm glad we're here for some other reason. It's far too hot out there for running and jumping. And there's no smooth ground. It's all cracks and tufts and hillocks."

Mrs Enders snorted disdainfully. "When I was your age," she said, "I had much more verve and energy. You can't give up because of a few cracks and a little sunshine."

"Anyway, I don't want to be an athlete," Peter retorted. "I want to be a vet."

"All the more reason for being really fit," said Mrs Enders. "It will help when you're wrestling elephants." She dropped her toast and cackled with laughter.

Peter scowled. Jean gave him a warning kick. She didn't think it was a good idea to annoy Granny Enders.

"The eggs are getting cold," she said. "Come and eat them, everyone!"

57

Amy pulled her chair to the table, her eyes fixed on Granny Enders' face. "Why are we really here?" she asked.

The old lady topped an egg neatly, with a blow of her spoon. "You may wonder," she said, "why I choose to live out here, in the back of beyond."

"Where exactly are we?" asked Jean.

"In Australia."

"But whereabouts in Australia?"

"Oh, somewhere in the middle," said Mrs Enders vaguely.

"But which state?" asked John.

Mrs Enders gave him an unfriendly glare. "Does it really matter? I have more important things to do than teach you geography."

John started to protest, but Mrs Enders hurried on. "As you know, I am very old, very old indeed. That's nothing! People like me can live for centuries. But about every seventy years, we need special herbs, specially prepared, to keep us fit and strong. In Europe these have become impossible to find — wiped out by herbicides and so on. You know about that."

"Of course we do. That's why you came to Australia with us in the first place," said Jean. "And you found the herbs — and, Granny, you look years younger!"

"Yes," said Mrs Enders, with a satisfied smile. "They are different plants, but have the same properties. They work well. Some, like the European herbs, have to be eaten fresh. But I also found some other Australian plants, even more

58

rare and marvellous. They keep their potency even when they are dried. They are so powerful I think they would last for ever. Now, I have friends all over the world in the same plight as I was. These new herbs could save us all."

"Where do the plants grow?" asked Amy eagerly.

"Here," said Mrs Enders. "That's the snag. They grow here and nowhere else. Some mystery in the soil, some subtlety in the climate. My Aboriginal friends have searched the outback for me. I have tried to sprout the seeds in a hundred similar places. They only flourish here, in a very small area. So here I must live . . . at least until I have stored supplies for the next few hundred years. The plants are too precious to be left for long, unguarded."

"You've made yourself very comfortable," said Jean, glancing around.

"Yes," said Mrs Enders. "I've converted this little old shack quite to my taste. But there's one big problem."

"Water!" said John.

"Water," echoed Mrs Enders. "I don't want nosy strangers delivering it in trucks. And why should I manage with tank water anyway? I like baths, good, deep baths!" Her voice was quite angry. "Come and look!" She pushed away her plate, jumped to her feet and strode out of the kitchen. The children followed curiously.

At the back of the house was a lean-to shed. Mrs Enders flung open the door.

The children peeped inside. The floor was covered with shining tiles and on them gleamed a huge, black marble bath. A matching wash basin stood in a corner. The taps and all the fittings were glittering gold.

"Useless!" mourned Mrs Enders. "All quite useless."

Candar leapt lightly up and stalked along the rim of the bath.

"You'd need hundreds of litres to fill this!" said John.

"I intend to have them," boomed Mrs Enders. "Sooner or later. One way or another."

"If you can make your own electricity," said Peter, "why can't you fix the water too?"

Mrs Enders snorted. "Electricity is child's play," she said. "Water is much more difficult."

"Can't Candar do anything?" asked Amy, tickling the little cat behind the ear.

"Cats," said Mrs Enders, "have no affinity for water. Have you ever tried to bath a cat?"

"I don't quite see how we can help," said Jean uneasily.

Mrs Enders looked at them thoughtfully, one after another. "Have you ever heard of water divining?" she asked.

"No," said Amy and John together.

"Yes, of course," said Jean. "Some people are supposed to be able to find underground water, with forked twigs or rods. They walk up and down holding the rod in front of them. And if there is water somewhere, the tip dips down toward it."

"Only it isn't true, of course," said Peter scornfully.

"Of course it's true," snapped Granny Enders. "Some people have a special gift."

"Can't you do it?" asked John, in surprise. "I'd have thought you could have done anything like that."

"Well, I can't!" muttered Mrs Enders. "Just as you, John, have no ear for music, I have no talent for water divining!" Then her voice softened. "On the other hand," she said, "my dear friend, your great-great-grandmother, had a remarkable gift. She could find water anywhere."

"Can Dad do it?" asked Peter.

"No he cannot!" said Mrs Enders sharply. "I had high hopes for him, when I took him in as a child. But he was a big disappointment. I've never known him do a single thing that was in the least out of the ordinary."

She paused and again stared at each of them in turn. "However, I shall be very surprised," she said, "if at least one of you hasn't inherited poor Isabel's gift. Surely one out of four!"

The children looked at one another.

A Strange Experiment

Granny Enders produced a springy, forked twig from behind the marble bath. She filled a shallow dish with water from the tank, and set it on the dusty ground behind the house.

"Amy first," ordered Mrs Enders. "Amy is the most likely one. There's a lot of Isabel in Amy."

But when Amy held the stick over the pan of water, it stayed lifeless in her hands. "It's no use," she said sadly at last. "It isn't moving at all."

"Let me try," said John, snatching the twig and dropping it in the pan.

Mrs Enders started and looked at it closely. "Did it twist? Did you feel it pull downwards?" she asked.

John hesitated. "No, I don't think so," he said unwillingly. He lifted up the forked stick and held it over the water.

"It's wobbling!" yelled Jean.

"No, it's me that's wobbling," said John. He tottered and sat down abruptly on the sand.

Mrs Enders looked at him without amusement. "We're trying to conduct a serious experiment," she said. "You next, Jean."

Jean took the twig by its forked tips and tried to remember a picture she had once seen. The diviner had kept his palms upwards, his elbows close to his sides. The twig must be flexed, held in a delicate balance. Slowly she walked towards the dish. Gently she moved the twig back and forward over the water.

"I can't feel anything at all," she sighed. "Here you are, Peter."

"I don't believe in it," said Peter. "We're wasting our time." He turned on his heel and started back towards the house.

"Peter!" cried Mrs Enders in a terrible voice. "Come back here at once and pick up that stick."

She looked so fierce that Peter thought it best not to argue. Shrugging, he walked to the water dish and picked up the twig.

"No, hold it like this!" snapped Mrs Enders. "Put your thumbs there!"

Peter was starting to feel angry at being ordered about. He looked deliberately bored as he held out the twig. When the feeling started in his hands, he thought he was imagining it. The stick seemed to be pressing against his thumbs. It twitched. It started to dip. He held it with all his strength, trying to control it. But the tip bent lower and lower, towards the dish of water. Frightened, he dropped it and jumped aside,

63

rubbing his tingling palms. Mrs Enders watched with glittering eyes.

"Were you pretending?" asked John.

"No," said Peter shakily. "No, it really moved. I felt it."

"Splendid!" said Mrs Enders. "Splendid! Try it again."

Again Peter stretched out the little branch over the pan of water. Again it dipped and twisted, almost breaking free of his grasp.

"You can do it!" cried Jean.

"Five minutes' rest," said Mrs Enders, "then you can start work, Peter. I want you to check every metre of ground, within half a kilometre."

All morning Peter walked slowly backwards and forwards over the sun-baked land. Mrs Enders found him an old, wide-brimmed straw hat, which he refused at first to wear. After half an hour in the heat, he was glad of it. The others took turns to walk with him, for company. Frequently they went back to the house for cool drinks in the shade of the verandah.

"You have masses of orange juice!" said John, pulling yet another bottle from the fridge.

"Orange juice is easy," said Mrs Enders. "But who wants to bath in orange juice?"

At one o'clock they had a hurried lunch. Then Peter started the endless pacing to and fro again. His arms ached from holding out the forked stick. His feet were hot and sore. His eyelids felt gritty.

"I can't go on much longer," he said to Amy, at three o'clock. "I'm so tired I could fall down and sleep for a week."

They were on the rim of a shallow hollow, about a hundred metres from the house. Peter hurled the twig away from him and sat down on the sand, huddled under the big hat.

"You've done enough for today," said Amy. "Let's go back and tell Granny Enders you need a rest."

"I'll just do a few more metres," said Peter, struggling to his feet. He walked across and picked up the forked twig. Wearily he began to pace across the hollow.

Then he stiffened. A force seemed to be flowing from the twig, into his hands, along his arms. Slowly, as he battled to hold it straight, the forked tip dipped towards the ground.

"Stay right there!" cried Amy. "I'll get the others." She ran as fast as she could towards the house, leaping over the clumps of spinifex, shouting for Mrs Enders.

Soon they were all out in the little hollow.

"Here?" asked Mrs Enders. "Are you sure? Right here? Show me!" Peter demonstrated with the twig.

"Yes!" shrieked Mrs Enders, very excited. "That's a very strong signal. There must be water under there. All I need to do is tap it."

"It might be a long way down," said Jean doubtfully. "You'll have to hire some men with a drilling rig."

"Nonsense!" said Mrs Enders briskly. "I refuse to have strangers nosing around. Candar and I can fix a simple thing like a pump."

The cat was sitting at the edge of the hollow. He shook the hot sand distastefully from his paws. "When you asked me out here, I believe you mentioned a holiday," he muttered sourly.

"You can have your holiday later on," said Granny Enders. "Now back to the house, children! Stay inside and don't look out of the windows. Shut the door and close the shutters."

"Why can't we watch?" asked John.

"Why can't you do as you're told?" snapped Granny Enders.

She looked so fierce that the children dared not argue. They hurried back to the house and closed the door behind them.

Shortly afterwards the noises began — rumblings, grindings, boomings, and a screech of metal on metal that set the children's teeth on edge. A red glow flickered through cracks in the old shutters.

"Whatever are they doing out there?" wondered Peter, pacing restlessly up and down. "It sounds as though they're ripping the place apart."

"She told us not to look, but she can't stop us listening," said Jean.

There was a final, awful crack or explosion, then complete silence. The children sat, straining their ears in the dim, shuttered room. Eventually there was a small scratching noise at the door.

Amy ran to open it. "Candar!" she cried. "You look dreadful!"

The cat stood swaying in the doorway, limp and bedraggled, his dark face and paws powdered with dust. He dragged himself across the carpet, collapsed under the fan, and seemed instantly to fall asleep.

"I wonder if Granny's all right!" exclaimed Amy. Without stopping to think, she ran out of the open door, across the sandy plain and over the little rise. More cautiously the others followed.

Granny Enders was sitting in the dip, her legs sprawled out on the sand. She looked weary, but nowhere near as exhausted as Candar.

The children stood and stared. After all the banging and crashing the hollow looked undisturbed. But in the middle of the dip sat an old-fashioned iron pump. It looked like something off a Christmas card, with a spout at the front and a long handle at the side.

"But don't you need one of those windmill things?" asked Peter.

"I can have what I like," said Mrs Enders, sounding a bit breathless. "And this is the sort of pump I like."

"Will it work?" asked John.

"Of course it will work!" said Granny Enders. "Do you think I've been wasting my time? Fetch me a bucket, child, and I'll show you whether it works or not."

John was soon back with the bucket. Mrs Enders placed it under the spout of the pump. "This," she gloated, "is a great occasion. Now I have my own water! Clean, sparkling, beautiful water — water for the teapot, water for the bath! Thank you all for your help. It is all most satisfactory."

She seized the handle and began to pump. For a few seconds nothing happened, then suddenly a stream of liquid shot from the spout. Peter gave a cheer. The others shouted with excitement. They all began to clap their hands. And then they faltered. Something was not quite right. That water looked and smelt most peculiar.

Faster and faster Mrs Enders pumped. The bucket brimmed and overflowed. And suddenly the old woman's expression changed. She bent over the bucket and glared into its depths. She dabbled her hand in the liquid, and sniffed her fingers. Then with a screech of rage she kicked at the bucket with all her strength, sending it halfway across the hollow, its contents soaking into the earth.

"Oil!" spat Mrs Enders. "Where is my lovely water? This is oil."

She was still in a huff hours later.

"Most people would be glad to find oil," suggested Jean nervously.

"Most people are nincompoops," snorted Granny Enders. "I have no use for the stuff. I can't take a bath in oil!"

"And your car doesn't use petrol," said Peter. He struggled to control himself for a minute, then burst out laughing. "I don't seem to be a very good water diviner."

"This is no laughing matter," growled Mrs Enders. "You'll have to try again, Peter!"

"Perhaps next time," said John, "it will be custard."

Plan Two

It was cold at night in that lonely place, but every morning the temperature soared. For two long days Peter walked and walked, back and forward in the hot sunshine.

At last Mrs Enders admitted defeat. "This place is as dry as a load of old bones. It's time to switch to Plan Two.

"What's Plan Two?" asked John.

"Rainmaking," said Mrs Enders. "Hm-mm . . . "

"If you can make it rain, you have no problem!" said Peter indignantly. "Why did I have to do all that divining?"

Mrs Enders scowled. "Once it begins to rain," she said, "I can keep it going. But I can't get it started by myself. And I've certainly tried! I've studied the subject for years. I've travelled all over the world, watching rainmaking ceremonies."

"Do they really work?" asked Jean.

"Sometimes they seem successful," said Granny Enders, "but it's very hard to tell. Maybe it would have rained anyway. There are all sorts of different rituals in different places. Some may work, some may be just mumbo-jumbo. I think I'd stand a better chance using lots of them all together. But there's only one of me, and that makes it difficult. Up to now I've had no success at all. And no cat will help you to make it rain. They'd sooner it didn't happen."

"How can we help?" asked Amy eagerly.

"Come outside and we'll make a start," said Granny Enders. "The situation is getting desperate." She herded the children on to the verandah. "Now I don't want the rain too close," she said. "Why do you think my special herbs grow here and nowhere else? Because the soil and the climate are just exactly right! It's a very delicate balance, and rain would upset things. The plants might not survive. It's too big a risk."

"Then what are we trying to do?" asked Jean, puzzled.

"Use your brains," said Granny Enders. "Look at that dry, empty creek. It only runs for a few weeks every year, when rain falls on the mountains over there. So we make it rain on the mountains. It's quite obvious."

"How do we start? What do we do?" asked Amy. She was greatly excited at the idea of rainmaking.

"First," said Mrs Enders, "it might be as well to change my dress." She walked back into the house. The children stood waiting.

"This is going to be a waste of time, you know," grumbled Peter. "There may be

71

something in water-divining, but rainmaking is sheer nonsense."

"You don't know!" protested Amy. "We haven't tried it yet."

"I wonder why she's changing her dress?" said Jean. "Perhaps she's going to dance around, and that flowing skirt would get in the way."

But when Mrs Enders reappeared, the new dress was even more billowy than the old one, a long, grey, voluminous gown, streaked with drops and drizzles of silver.

"You look like a rainy day!" said John.

Jean held her breath and waited for an explosion, but Mrs Enders seemed pleased with this tactless remark.

"That's just the idea, John," she said. "You can't be as stupid as you sometimes appear."

"Are we going to begin now?" asked Amy breathlessly.

"Be quiet for a minute and let me think," commanded Mrs Enders. She shut her eyes and frowned fiercely. "Now where shall we start? I think we can dispense with sacrifices — slaughtering animals and so on."

"Yes, let's not do that!" said Jean.

"You get a fine dramatic effect," said Mrs Enders, "but I find it disagreeable, and I'm sure it doesn't work."

"Good!" chorused the children.

"I shall sit on the verandah," said Granny Enders, "and concentrate on the mountains. If the rain comes, it's essential it falls over there.

72

You are the ones who will have to bring the clouds."

"How are we supposed to do that?" asked Peter crossly.

"Someone should be dressed up in leaves and flowers," said Mrs Enders. "It had better be Amy. Hurry up and find some suitable plants!"

But there did not seem to be much around that was suitable. Small, scratchy leaves and prickly berries were all that the children could find. Jean knotted them on to a string and Amy placed it gingerly round her neck.

"I suppose that will have to do," said Mrs Enders. "Now take a bucket of water, and all of you walk along the bed of the creek. And at every bend, sprinkle Amy with water."

The children trudged along the bed of the creek. Amy quite enjoyed all the sprinkling. It kept her cooler than the others. But the "necklace" made her skin itch furiously.

"That was a sheer waste of water," muttered Peter, tipping the last drops over his sister's head. "The tank will soon be empty, if we keep splashing it about."

They went back to the house. Mrs Enders was sitting on a rocking chair on the verandah, cracking her jewelled knuckles and staring at the mountains. The sky over the distant peaks was still a glaring blue.

"I'll give you all different things to do," said Mrs Enders. She rummaged in her pocket and pulled out an oyster shell lined with mother-of-pearl. "Jean, take this! I want you to scrape a little powder from the shell, mix it with water and bury it in the ground. And all the time you are doing it, sing a little song, calling the rain."

"Wouldn't I need the proper words?" asked Jean.

"We don't have the proper words," snapped Mrs Enders. "I'm no linguist! Just do your best."

Next she produced a piece of paper and handed it to Amy, who had gratefully removed her scratchy wreath and thrown it away. "Now this is said to be a very powerful symbol. Find a nice flat patch of sand and make a drawing of it."

"I'm not very good at drawing," said Amy.

"Nonsense," said Mrs Enders. "Anyone could draw that, just a lot of wavy lines and patterns. And you'd better sing something appropriate, while you're doing it. Use your imagination."

"It's no good telling me to sing," said Peter flatly. "I can't and I won't!"

Mrs Enders fixed him with a hard, glinting eye. "If I tell you to sing," she said, "you'll sing like a bellbird. But for the time being here is something more to your taste." She tossed a box of matches to Peter. "Make a little hollow and fill it with water. Build a tiny fire, then put it out by sprinkling drops of water from the hollow over the flames. Then build the fire again and make me some good clouds of smoke: clouds of smoke that look like rain clouds."

"Can I help with that?" asked John eagerly.

"No," said Mrs Enders. "You go and squat in

74

the dry creek and pretend you're a swamp frog, calling for rain. Let me hear you make a noise like a swamp frog!"

"I don't know how," protested John, very annoyed at this undignified role.

"Like this, like this!" said Granny Enders, leaning forward. She began to make loud, croaking noises.

Peter hooted with laughter, but stopped abruptly as she glared at him. "This is a serious matter," she said. "For all we know, swamp frogs could be absolutely vital. Now let's hear you, John!"

It was some time before she was satisfied. John stood next to the rocking chair, making various croaking noises, while the others fought desperately to stop themselves laughing. At last he managed a note which pleased the old woman, and she sent him towards the creek.

For hours the children did everything they were asked. As soon as they finished one strange task, Granny Enders suggested another.

"Peter, take this axe and cut a gash in the trunk of that little, stunted tree. Imagine you are releasing a wind that has been imprisoned in the trunk."

Peter raised his eyebrows, but took the axe. It was never worth arguing with Mrs Enders.

"Amy, dance round and round the tree and sing:
       'We call the wind,
       We call the rain!'"

The thing the children most enjoyed was sitting in a circle, trying to imitate the sound of a rainstorm. Peter played a flute. Jean and Amy tapped sticks in various rhythms. John, to his delight, was allowed to bang on a sort of drum, made by pegging a piece of leather taut over a hollow in the ground. They became quite proud of the effects they could produce: the sound of wind, the light patter of rain, then the loud drumming of a deluge. Carried away by enthusiasm, John pounded his drum and croaked loudly, like a swamp frog.

"Very good . . . very good!" shouted Mrs Enders.

"It's a shame none of it's working," muttered Peter into his flute.

But in the evening, just before sunset, when they had almost given up hope, a small dark cloud appeared over the mountains. They sat on the verandah and watched lightning flicker over the peaks.

"Splendid! Splendid!" cried Mrs Enders, rocking faster and faster in her chair. "I can keep it going now, with just half an hour's effort a day. What a pity we don't know which of those rituals worked! Another time I really must sort it out."

Next morning the weather was as hot as ever, the sky as blue. But over that one particular spot on the mountains, the tiny cloud still hung, gently and steadily raining.

In a few days the creek was full of sparkling water. The banks began to sprout with tiny

blades of green. The children could see no pipes, but suddenly water ran from the taps in the house: cold from the cold taps, mysteriously hot from the hot ones. Mrs Enders spent long hours singing in the bathroom, great clouds of steam drifting through cracks in the door.

Not far from the house the creek filled a hollow with water before snaking on its way over the plain. The children used this as a swimming hole, and the days passed very pleasantly. Only Jean was occasionally troubled by thoughts of home. Granny Enders, satisfied with her arrangements at last, seemed to have forgotten they had a home to go to, and had apparently no plans for ending their visit. But then, Jean thought, Granny never did talk much about her plans.

Unwelcome Visitors

Late one morning, when the sun was high and hot, two very weary men came staggering over the plain. Their tongues were dry, their eyes were bloodshot. Their bodies ached all over.

"Call yourself a pilot?" croaked one. "You're a blithering fool! We're going to die out here."

"We should have stayed with the plane," said the other, doing his best not to blither. "That way, they might have found us."

"It wouldn't have helped at all," said the first man. "You crashed right into that gully. The wreck is covered with scrub. No chance of anyone spotting it there. They wouldn't even look hereabouts. We must have been way off course. You managed to lose us before you crashed us."

"Sorry Alec!" said the second man, for the fifth time that morning. And then he suddenly gave a yell of joy. "Look! Look! A shack! We're saved!"

"It can't be a shack," said Alec. "No one in their senses would live out here. It's just a squarish rock. You'll see."

But as they drew nearer, it became plain that

they *were* looking at a little timber cottage.

"It'll be a ruin of course," said Alec. "But at least we can get out of the sun." The men broke into a stumbling run.

"Good grief! That's some sort of a pump," gasped Jack, as they came closer. "It'd have to be dry!"

The children were preparing lunch, under Mrs Enders' directions, when they heard the bang on the door. John opened it.

Alec and Jack stared past him into the kitchen, dumbfounded.

"It's a mirage," gasped Jack.

"Or a dream," murmured Alec. "A nasty-tasting dream. What's that stuff in your pump, lady? I took a gulp and nearly poisoned myself. Lucky that creek was nearby. I must've swallowed a bucket of water and I still have a nasty taste in my mouth. Horrible black stuff, it is."

"Oh, I'm sorry," said John. "That isn't water. It's oil."

Mrs Enders drew herself up. She was looking most annoyed. "We don't welcome visitors here," she said.

"Hold on, lady," gasped Jack. "We're lost. You wouldn't turn a dog away, in a place like this."

"Lost?" snapped Mrs Enders. "Two grown men, lost?" Then she seemed to take in their bedraggled appearance. "Oh, very well," she said ungraciously. "Come in."

Alec and Jack sat down, dusty and exhausted, at the kitchen table. They gratefully accepted tea and sandwiches. As they ate, Mrs Enders questioned them closely, snorting derisively at every turn of the story.

"Well, it can't be helped," she said at last. "But you can't stay here. I'll run you over to the road and you can hitch a lift."

"Where are we exactly, then?" asked Jack, munching his cheese and tomato sandwich. "I really lost my bearings before we crashed."

"You are here," said Mrs Enders. "And I shall be delighted when you are somewhere else."

The men looked at her, puzzled.

"What I mean to say . . ." said Jack, "if you take us to this road you mention, and someone gives us a lift . . . where will that someone be going?"

"You'll find out when you get there, won't you?" said Mrs Enders. "I'll just put on my driving shoes." She swept out of the kitchen.

"That pump out there, with the oil," whispered Alec to the children, "what's the story about that? Who fixed it up?"

"Oh, Granny Enders put in the pump by herself, last week," said John. "She thought she would get water. The creek was dry."

"Last week? By herself? That old girl? How could she fix up something like that?"

"Go and see if Granny is ready, John," said Jean hastily, pushing her young brother towards

81

the door. She had a feeling that the less they said to Jack and Alec the better.

But at that moment Mrs Enders reappeared. She was frowning. "Where can he be? Come on children! Help me look for Candar. I can't drive the car until I find that cat."

The children trudged around in the hot sunshine, calling and looking for Candar. He was not in the shade of the back verandah; he was not on the hot, tin roof, nor chasing beetles on the dusty plain. Candar obviously had no intention of being found. But at last Mrs Enders noticed a dappled shape in the shadow of a small, scrubby bush, and the cat followed them reluctantly back to the shack.

As they approached the open door they heard voices. Granny Enders put her finger to her lips. They all crept up to the shack, their feet making no noise on the sand.

"There's something funny about the whole set-up," Jack was saying. "That rude old woman gives me the creeps. I don't know why. What's she doing out here with a brood of kids? And this house doesn't make sense. Just look at all this gear! I think I'm dreaming. Pinch me Alec. Ow! Not that hard!"

"Oh, she's just a rich, batty old bird," scoffed Alec, "playing games, keeping house in the desert. But that oil . . . now there's something interesting. I'll bet she doesn't own the mineral rights to that gully. We could move in on that oil under her nose. As soon as we're back in town I'll

82

check it out. There's a fortune to be made here, Jack, or I'm a lizard!''

Mrs Enders shook with fury. She waved the children back, away from the shack. They retreated behind the water tank where they could speak freely, out of earshot of the men.

"You see how my hospitality is repaid!" raged Mrs Enders. "I will not have it!"

"But you don't want the oil anyway," said Peter.

"I don't want strangers here either," growled Mrs Enders, "tearing up the desert, destroying my precious plants. Oh dear no! Something will have to be done!"

"Perhaps if you explained to them," said Jean, "they might change their minds."

"Why should I explain? It's none of their business," snapped Mrs Enders. "And what would they care for my explanations? They're only interested in money!"

"Couldn't you magic the oil away?" asked Amy.

"No," said Granny. "Too complicated by far. I'm no geologist. Besides, it wouldn't stop those wretches looking — "

"Well, you're a witch!" interrupted John mischievously. "Why don't you turn them into frogs?"

Granny Enders looked thoughtful. The other children stared at her, horrified.

"John!" exclaimed Amy.

"You can't do that!" said Peter.

"That would be a *dreadful* thing to do!" cried Jean.

"Yes," mused Mrs Enders, smiling to herself. "But it would be very satisfying! Stay here!"

She strode quickly to the kitchen door and looked in. "Do either of you young men have wives, or children?" she enquired pleasantly.

"No," replied Jack, looking puzzled.

"No. Why?" asked Alec suspiciously.

"Ah, just a friendly interest," said Mrs Enders. "I suppose, however, you have mothers and fathers? Brothers and sisters?"

"I'm an orphan myself," said Jack.

"Don't bother much with the family. We never saw eye to eye," said Alec. "Haven't seen them in years."

"How very convenient!" said Mrs Enders. She stepped into the kitchen and closed the door firmly behind her.

The children stood looking at each other.

"She wouldn't, would she?" whispered Jean.

"She couldn't, could she?" muttered Peter. John was very pale.

Everything was very quiet in the shack. They strained their ears. Minutes passed.

At last John could bear it no longer. He ran to the door and wrenched it open. The others followed.

Mrs Enders was standing by the kitchen table. On it sat a pair of large, dazed-looking lizards.

"Oh," cried Jean in horror, clapping her hands to her mouth. The children crept up to the table and looked carefully at the lizards. They were perfect, from their beady eyes to the tips of their scaly tails. No-one could think of anything to say.

"Now, we must keep the doors shut," said Mrs Enders briskly. "They mustn't get away. Come outside all of you, and help me build a cage. There's some chicken wire and planks under the tank."

It took the children most of the day to enclose part of the back verandah, to make a cage. Their hands were scratched with the chicken wire. John had a splinter in his finger and Peter had hammered his thumb. Mrs Enders did none of the hard work, but she scattered sand inside the run and arranged a few artistic pebbles. She also supplied a bowl of drinking water.

"Do you have to put them in a cage?" asked Jean, tweaking the splinter from John's finger.

"Of course," replied Mrs Enders. "When I have finished here, and they can do no more harm, I shall turn them back into men. I have to be able to find them. One lizard looks very like another."

They went back into the kitchen. Candar had herded the lizards into a corner by the fridge. He was patting their noses with his paw.

"Candar!" exclaimed Mrs Enders. "You should be ashamed of yourself! Stop behaving like a cat."

Candar shrugged with embarrassment, leapt on to the refrigerator and looked haughtily down at the children.

Granny Enders scooped up the lizards,

whisked them outside and placed them in the cage. After a while the creatures seemed to revive a little. They moved cautiously around, exploring their new home.

"They must be dreadfully unhappy!" said Jean, peering through the chicken wire.

"They're nothing of the sort," snapped Mrs Enders. "They have everything a lizard could require."

"But what must they be thinking?" wailed Amy.

"Lizards don't think," said Mrs Enders. "At least, not so that you would notice it."

"But these aren't really lizards," objected Peter.

"Of course they are," said Granny Enders. "When I transmogrify, I transmogrify properly!"

Home Again

The children were helping Granny Enders to prepare her herbs. They had gathered the plants and tied them in bunches to hang on strings along the verandah. Now, when the little leaves were dry and brittle, they were gently rubbing them from the spiky twigs.

"Careful, John," warned Jean. "You nearly knocked over that jar. This is the last batch, Granny. We've nearly finished."

"Yes," gloated Mrs Enders. "A much better crop than I hoped! Another season should provide all that I need. Enough for me, enough for all my friends . . . for the next five hundred years at any rate."

"It is time for me to leave," said Candar, who was sitting on the edge of the kitchen table. "I should have been in Fiji for the last full moon. And I'm due in Alaska on the twenty-seventh." He leapt to the floor and prowled restlessly up and down. Mrs Enders looked offended.

"Well if you must, you must," she said. "But first we must take the children home."

"Can we go soon?" asked John eagerly. He

thought longingly of his friends in Sydney and the games they must be playing without him.

"Very soon," said Mrs Enders, sticking a label with mysterious symbols on to the last of her jars.

"Couldn't we stay just a little bit longer?" asked Amy sadly.

"Come now, Amy, all things come to an end," said Mrs Enders. But her voice was kind.

"How about the rain?" asked Peter. "Won't the rain stop if you're not here to keep it going?"

"And who's going to feed the . . . er . . . lizards?" asked Jean.

"Do stop making a fuss!" said Mrs Enders. "I've been giving it all some thought and there's no real problem. We shall just have to go back to last week."

The children looked at her, baffled. "Whatever do you mean, Granny?" asked Jean.

Mrs Enders spoke slowly and carefully, as if explaining something very simple to someone very stupid. "Today is Tuesday. If we start on our journey today, the rain will stop tomorrow. But if we set off *last* Tuesday, I can be back in plenty of time for tomorrow."

There was a long silence.

"But that's crazy," said Peter at last. "Even if you could do it, it wouldn't work. If we had gone home last Tuesday, we wouldn't have been here to make it rain last Wednesday."

"We can't spend last week travelling home," said Jean. "We already spent it here."

Mrs Enders drew herself up to her full height

and glared at the children. "Don't try to tell ME what is possible!" she said. "At times like this I see how much you take after your tedious father. The whole thing is much simpler than you imagine. Adjustments can be made. Details can be altered. Time is full of twiddles. Just do what you're told, and don't answer back! Now go and pack your cases."

Hurriedly the children did as they were ordered. When they came back into the living room Mrs Enders was wearing a flowing, red cloak. She had pushed all the furniture against one wall, and was drawing a huge circle on the floor, with a big, black, felt-tipped pen.

"Granny" cried Jean. "What are you doing? You'll ruin the carpet! That ink will never come off."

The old woman took no notice. While they watched she drew symbols all around the circle — different geometric shapes; others that resembled plants, birds and animals. Candar stalked around examining everything she did. He had lost his usual supercilious calm. He seemed excited.

"Now, everyone come inside the circle," ordered Granny Enders. "And bring your cases with you. Sit down and join hands." The children crouched on the floor, not knowing what to expect. Mrs Enders sat in the middle, with Candar on her knee.

Over their heads the big, circular fan turned slowly, and then faster and faster. The cool breeze became a whirling wind. Amy's hair whipped across her cheeks. Peter's shirt billowed like a balloon. Suddenly they felt that the floor too was spinning. The circle was revolving, slowly at first, but gathering speed. Soon they were swinging so fast that everything looked blurred. The children felt sick and dizzy. They shut their eyes and held desperately to each other's hands. Then just as John felt he could not stand the spinning for one moment longer, they began to slow down.

"Open your eyes," said Mrs Enders briskly. "It is now last week."

Cautiously the children looked about them. The room seemed just the same. Overhead the fan turned gently. The ink had disappeared from the carpet.

Peter ran to the window and looked out. The plain simmered as usual in the sun. "How do we know it's last week?" he asked doubtfully.

"The creek!" cried Amy, beside him. "Look at the creek!"

The dry channel wound past the shack, littered with bleached pebbles; not a drop of shining water between the parched banks.

"Into the car, everyone!" said Mrs Enders. "We must start at once."

"I suppose it all falls on me again," grumbled Candar. He sprang on to the verandah rail and looked with disdain at the purple car.

"It is a great happiness," said Mrs Enders, "to use one's talents in the service of others."

The cat eyed her sourly. "It would be a greater

90

happiness," he muttered, "to have a rest from this sort of thing."

"Hadn't we better feed the lizards, before we go?" asked Jean.

"It's last week, child," said Granny Enders. "The lizards have not yet arrived. No need to worry about them. I shall be back by yesterday, at the latest."

She strode across to the car and opened the bonnet. Candar jumped inside and settled down.

Soon they were on their way. It was not like the outward trip, which had mostly seemed like ordinary motoring. Somehow night and day became blurred. There were no stops for meals or exercise, but they didn't feel hungry or thirsty or cramped, just overwhelmingly drowsy. Sometimes they slept. Sometimes they lay back in the velvet seats in a pleasant daze. Jean kept trying to concentrate, but couldn't remember on what, or why. Peter, half asleep, wondered idly how fast they were driving. Trees and buildings flickered past the windows like speeding shadows. John did not fight the drowsiness. He slept in a corner of the back seat, curled up in a ball.

Amy lay back in a trance. It seemed too much effort even to speak, but at last she managed to say: "Why are we so sleepy, Granny?"

"It's time lag," said Mrs Enders. "You're just not used to time travel. You should be over it by the time I have you home."

Candar is Offended

Peter yawned, uncurled and looked out of the window. Dawn was just breaking and the shadowy streets looked very familiar. "Wake up, Amy, John, Jean! We're nearly there." The others rubbed their eyes. It was quite true. There was the post office. There was the supermarket. In a few minutes they would be home.

"We must have been asleep for a very long time," said Jean.

"It depends how you measure it," said Mrs Enders.

She turned the car into their street, then stopped abruptly. A deep trench ran the length of the road, surrounded by piles of earth and little red lamps.

"They're digging up the sewer," said John. "Or perhaps the gas pipes."

"This is outrageous!" fumed Mrs Enders. "I refuse to leave the car so far from the house. It's unthinkable!"

Amy looked at her sympathetically. Granny was tired and irritable, after the journey. All the time they had been sleeping, she had been driving.

"There's nothing else we can do," said Peter, craning his neck. "We can't take it any closer."

"There's always something else one can do," snapped Mrs Enders. "But it's an infernal nuisance. Out of the car everyone, and take your luggage out of the boot."

She climbed from her seat and opened the bonnet, to release Candar.

"Good morning," said the cat. He sprang to the pavement and lazily stretched his legs, admiring the length of his claws.

He doesn't look tired, thought Amy. He looks as though he'd had a good sleep, just like us. She turned to watch Mrs Enders, who was standing in the gutter, scowling at the car.

"I should like a newspaper," said the old woman unexpectedly. She rummaged in a hidden pocket and pulled out a few coins. "Run along and buy me one, children!"

"But the shop won't be open," said Jean. "It's only just getting light."

"Newsagents keep peculiar hours," said Granny Enders. "They get up very early."

"Not as early as this!" said Peter.

Mrs Enders' bony nose started to quiver and her lips became a thin line.

"Give me the money," said Jean hurriedly. "You never know. I'll just run round the corner and have a look."

"You will *all* go!" thundered Granny Enders.

Amy and John left hastily. Jean grabbed the coins and followed. Peter suddenly remembered what had happened to the two men in the desert,

93

and hurried after the others. They met no one as they walked. The street was quite deserted.

"There!" said Peter. "I told her it would be closed." The newsagent's was locked and barred, with no sign of activity. The children turned and walked back towards home.

They found Granny Enders where they had left her. Candar was toying with something in the gutter, patting it with his slender paws.

"Where's the car?" asked Peter, staring around.

"Look!" said Amy, in a shaky voice, pointing to the cat. He was playing with a tiny model car. It was only six centimetres high, and perfect in every detail.

"But that's just a toy," said John.

He bent forward to pick up the little car, but Mrs Enders was faster. She whisked the toy into her pocket. "Come along," she said briskly. "I need some breakfast."

The house was silent, the blinds closed, the front door locked. "Has anyone got a key?" demanded Mrs Enders.

When the children said no, she rang the bell loudly, then seized the brass knocker and began a tremendous banging. A startled shout came from inside, and shortly afterwards Mr Pitt appeared, blinking, in his pyjamas.

"Good heavens!" he said. "I thought it must be the police, or a national disaster or something. Did you have to bang like that, Granny?"

"You should have been up to welcome us!"

snapped Mrs Enders. "You always were incredibly lazy, George."

"What's happening? Is something the matter?" Mrs Pitt's worried voice floated out from the bedroom.

Granny Enders stalked into the hall. "I've brought back your family, at great trouble and expense. The least you can do is offer me some breakfast!"

Mrs Pitt was so relieved and pleased to see the children that she ignored Mrs Enders' rudeness, and bustled about in her dressing-gown, preparing breakfast. She had waited every day for a letter with Granny Enders' address. "We should never have let her take them off into the wilds," she had said to her husband, over and over again. "What could we have been thinking of? What came over us?"

Soon they were all eating hungrily. Candar nibbled at some sardines, but sneered at a saucer of cold milk.

"He likes cream," whispered Amy to her mother.

"So do we all," laughed Mrs Pitt, "but we don't feed cats on cream!"

Candar's ears gave an angry twitch.

In between mouthfuls, the children tried to answer questions from Mr and Mrs Pitt. It was not very easy. They did not know where they had been and they could not mention half the things that had happened.

"And how about the athletics training,

Granny?" asked Mrs Pitt. "Did the children do well?"

"Athletics training?" queried Mrs Enders. "Whatever can you mean, Brenda?"

"You said you were going to coach the children," said Mr Pitt. "You mentioned the Olympics!"

Mrs Enders seemed astounded. "I ask you," she exclaimed, "is that very likely? Have you both taken leave of your senses? What would I know about such things, an old woman like me?"

"But I'm sure you said . . ." faltered Mrs Pitt.

"Are you trying to make fun of me?" shouted Granny Enders. "Are you mocking a frail old lady? Well, I don't find such jokes amusing!"

Mr Pitt thought it was best to change the subject. He looked wildly around and his eye fell upon Candar.

"It's nice to see the puss again," he said, "but isn't he a nuisance when you're travelling?"

"Oh, I don't mind the fuss," said Mrs Enders, calming down. "We must all look after our pets."

"You should keep him on a lead," said Mrs Pitt. "It would be safer. They have some nice little harnesses and leads at the pet shop."

A wicked gleam flickered in Mrs Enders' eye. "What a good idea!" she said.

Candar lifted his head from the saucer and stared at her, outraged. Then he jumped swiftly on to the windowsill and turned his back on the room.

Mrs Enders sat back in her chair and roared

with laughter. She seemed in a high good humour for the rest of the meal.

"Will you be staying for a while, Granny?" asked Mrs Pitt nervously.

"Certainly not," said Mrs Enders. "I can't spare this family any more of my time. Candar and I will be leaving later today."

A snort came from the windowsill. The cat sat with hunched shoulders. He appeared to be sulking.

After breakfast Mr and Mrs Pitt went off to shower and get dressed. The children lingered at the table, happy to be home.

"We'll start back after lunch," said Mrs

Enders to Candar. The cat turned round and glanced coldly at her. The children could see he was still offended.

"You," he said, "may go where you please. I have to attend to my own concerns."

Mrs Enders looked quite taken aback. "But I need you to drive the car." Her voice became sugary sweet. "Just the one short trip, my dear, and then you can do as you like."

"I can do as I like *right now*," said Candar disdainfully. "Harness indeed! You must make your own way home this time." He leapt to the floor, stalked out of the room and began to scratch furiously at the front door.

"Can't you take a little joke?" shouted Mrs Enders. "Cats have no sense of humour!"

The children went hastily out into the hall.

"I'm sure she didn't mean it about the lead," said Jean.

"She was only joking," said John.

"Please be so good as to open the front door," said the cat frostily.

Peter twisted the latch. "Goodbye, then," he said.

Candar paused for a moment on the doorstep and Amy bent to stroke his silky head. "Will you ever come back, Candar?"

"I might, if it suits me," said the cat. "Or then again, I might not." He pressed his head briefly against her hand, then streaked away down the garden path, and out of the front gate.

The children went back into the kitchen. Mrs

Enders was sitting bolt upright at the table. On the cloth before her sat the model car. She was glaring at it in exasperation.

"How will you get home then?" asked Amy timidly.

"Are you going to use a broom again?" suggested Jean.

The old woman scowled. "Too much traffic," she said. "Too many aeroplanes. Worse than when I was here before. You seem to be right in the flight path."

"Why not catch a plane yourself?" said John.

"Or a bus or a train?" said Peter, "like ordinary people do."

"There are plenty of different ways to travel," said Granny Enders, reaching for the coffeepot. She poured the hot liquid so furiously that it splashed right out of the cup. "Candar can go and chase his tail."

Goodbye, Granny Enders

After breakfast Mrs Enders flung herself on the sofa. The waterbed had gone. Mrs Pitt had found its owner, after forty-seven phone calls.

"I need to sleep and must not be disturbed," said Granny Enders.

One hour passed, then two, then three, then four. The Pitts ate lunch but did not dare to wake the old woman. The children tiptoed about the house or wandered aimlessly in the garden, waiting for something to happen.

At last, late in the afternoon, when they were all in the kitchen, Mrs Enders reappeared. She was wearing her cloak and had an envelope in her hand. "Has anyone a stamp?" she asked pleasantly.

"Yes, I think so," replied Mrs Pitt. "There should be some in the drawer over there. Get one for Granny, John."

John quickly found the stamp. Mrs Enders thanked him graciously, licked it and began to stick it on the envelope. Then suddenly her expression changed. She ripped the stamp off again and glared at the little piece of paper.

"Flowers!" she said in disgust. "Whatever happened to the Queen?"

Mr Pitt looked up from his newspaper. "The stamps have been like that for quite a while, Granny."

Mrs Enders looked quite disconcerted. "Are there no stamps with people on them?" she demanded.

"The special stamps have all sorts of things on them," said Peter. "I'll show you my collection." He fetched his large, red album from the bedroom and opened it at the page for Australia.

"Not all those stamps have been used," said Mrs Enders, looking over his shoulder.

"No," said Peter. "Sometimes I buy them new."

The old lady pointed to a stamp with a picture of two little cricketers. Underneath the figures it said: "Australia. Test Cricket Centenary."

"Now that's the sort of stamp I like. That will do nicely," said Mrs Enders, and she plucked the stamp neatly from the page.

"But you'll spoil my collection," protested Peter. "It doesn't matter what sort of stamp goes on your letter."

"It matters to me!" said Granny Enders fiercely.

"Dad . . . make her give it back!"

Mr Pitt peered nervously round his newspaper. "You can probably get a swap at school," he said.

"Of course you can," said Granny Enders, as

101

she stuck the stamp firmly on the envelope. "Jean, I want you to post this for me tonight. I'll leave it on the hall table."

"You've forgotten to address the envelope," said John, looking at the blank white square.

"Forgotten?" snorted Mrs Enders. "Of course I haven't forgotten. I never forget anything."

"But I can't see any writing," said John.

"Of course you can't," snapped Granny Enders. "This ink takes time to mature."

"But how will the post office know where to send the letter?" asked Jean in surprise.

"By the time they need to know," said Granny, "the address will be there. In the meantime no one can poke his or her nose into my affairs. Now don't forget, Jean! Post this tonight. But don't put it into the box until just before the collection time. There's no sense in dragging things out." She swept out into the hall and did not come back.

"Invisible ink!" mused Mrs Pitt. "Granny gets more and more peculiar! And what did she mean by that last remark? It didn't seem to make any sense."

"She had her cloak on!" said Mr Pitt suddenly, ten minutes later. "Surely she hasn't left without saying goodbye!" He opened the door but the hall was empty. He hurried to the front door and opened that, but there was no one in the front garden.

The children searched the house and the four corners of the garden. Peter went down to the end of the road, looking in all directions. Mrs Enders had completely disappeared.

"She's gone home!" said Mrs Pitt crossly. "She didn't say a single word. She just went. She really is the rudest person I've ever met!"

As they walked into the house, Jean saw the letter, lying on the hall table, and glanced at the clock. "I can just catch the post with that, if I hurry," she said.

She picked up the envelope and ran quickly down the road. As she reached the mailbox a few drops of rain began to fall. I mustn't let it get wet, she thought.

She lifted her hand and popped the letter into the slot. And just as it slipped from her fingers into the box, she noticed the stamp. One of the tiny figures had a very familiar face.

"But are you sure?" asked Peter, later. "Perhaps you just imagined it."

"Absolutely one hundred per cent sure!" said Jean, still shaken. "She winked at me. What an awful way to travel."

"She'll be all right," said Amy. Then she smiled. "I wonder if I could do that?"

"You'd better not try!" said her sister grimly.

"I see why she left a broom by her mailbox," said John. He laughed. "I wonder if she gets ink on her nose from the franking machine."

"Well I don't suppose she'll be back," said Peter. "Not unless it suits her. Not unless she needs more help."

"She might come back for this," said John. He

pulled the little purple car from his pocket and spun the wheels with his finger. It was hard to believe it was not an ordinary toy.

"I'm sure she likes us really," said Amy, staring at her ring. "She's just not the sort of person who shows it."

And for a split second, in the depths of the red stone, she thought she saw someone smiling.